The
Neglected
Majority

The Neglected Majority

Dale Parnell

THE COMMUNITY COLLEGE PRESS
A division of the American Association
of Community and Junior Colleges

Copyright September, 1985
Second printing, 1986
Printed in the U.S.A.

Published by the Community College Press, a
division of the American Association of Community
and Junior Colleges, The National Center for
Higher Education, 1 Dupont Circle, Suite 410, N.W.,
Washington, D.C. 20036.

ISBN 0-87117-154-6

A nation that draws too broad a difference between its scholars and its warriors will have its thinking being done by cowards and its fighting by fools.

Thucydides

CONTENTS

FIGURES

FOREWORD

FEW OBSERVERS of the American educational scene may speak from the breadth of experience and depth of knowledge about education as Dale Parnell. High-school teacher, principal, school superintendent, state superintendent of public instruction, college professor, president of three community colleges, and for the past several years President and Chief Executive Officer of the American Association of Community and Junior Colleges, Dale Parnell is in a unique position to assess the effectiveness of education in our nation. In this valuable new book he clearly defines a weakness in our basic approach to education: the lack of a rigorous, constructive, and focused program of study to prepare the sixty to seventy percent of our high-school students who will not likely be pursuing a baccalaureate-degree program. It is important to help all students make a more significant contribution to our increasingly complex economy and have more enlightened participation in our free society. These students must not be *the neglected majority* of our eductional system as we enter the twenty-first century.

As one solution for the problem, Parnell proposes what he has termed a tech-prep/associate-degree four-year program. Commencing with the eleventh grade and concluding with the associate degree at the end of the sophomore year in a community, technical, or junior college, the tech-prep/associate-degree program is intended to run parallel to existing college-prep/baccalaureate-degree programs. Consisting of both vocational and liberal arts courses, the Parnell-designed course of study rests on a solid foundation of math, science, communications, and technology courses—all in an applied setting.

High school students who select the tech-prep/associate degree would do so in their junior year, just as some now elect a college-prep/baccalaureate-degree program; they would remain a part of the highly structured and focused program for the following four years. The tech-prep students would be taught by high school teachers in the eleventh and twelfth grades but have access to the faculty and facilities of the community, technical, or junior college when needed. Says Parnell, "Starting with a solid base of applied science, applied math, literacy courses, and technical programs, the high-school portion of the career program would be intentionally preparatory in nature. The tech-prep approach, built around career clusters and technical systems, would help students to develop broad-based competence in a career field while avoiding the pitfalls of receiving short-term and narrowly delineated job training."

Where would the tech-prep students come from? First of all, from that two-out-of-three students now enrolled in the general education or vocational education high-school tracks. Parnell reminds us that over half of the entering freshmen in *all* institutions of higher learning now begin their college careers in community, technical, or junior colleges, and that roughly eighty percent of the adult population in our nation do not hold college bachelor's degrees.

Parnell makes a convincing case for the argument that the complex, technological world of the future is really already here. The emerging truth is that higher and more comprehensive skills must be developed, particularly by the middle two quartiles of the work force. Tasks once reserved for baccalaureate-degree or advanced-degree holders must be assumed by those with fewer years of education and training, and all workers must continue to learn throughout their careers to remain useful. Technology, as it becomes more commercial, will increase America's need for middle-range proficiencies.

But the tech-prep/associate-degree program can never be born without a close and continuing interchange between the high school and college governing boards, key executive officers, and key faculty members. Such an interchange must lead to specific agreements on unified curricular programs that begin in grade eleven and continue without interruption through the associate degree. The chapter on the high-school/community college connection is must reading for every high-school and community college policymaker and leader. Parnell describes a number of such cooperative programs already under way throughout the country. It is exciting to read about them, and it is a privilege to commend this insightful new publication to your reading. Meeting the educational needs of *The Neglected Majority* is central to the future of America.

Thomas A. Shannon, *Executive Director*
National School Boards Association
Alexandria, Virginia

An Open Letter to the Leaders of American High Schools and Community Colleges

Dear Colleagues:

American education is undergoing constant reform. If reports and studies alone could improve schools and colleges, we would have achieved excellence in education a long time ago. Led by the clarion call to the American people, *A Nation at Risk*, the report from the National Commission on Excellence in Education, at least fifteen major reform reports and a host of others have been issued over the past twenty-four months calling for substantive changes in the American education system. Most of the recommendations are familiar: better teachers, a return to the basics, greater accountability, more time on tasks, better discipline, more courses in this and fewer in that, longer school years, more effective use of technology in education.

With so many education reform reports coming so fast, it would be easy to grow cynical—to say "These too will pass." But such an attitude will result in the loss of a tremendous opportunity. Never has the public been so conditioned to think seriously about education. Never have educators been more willing to give up some of their "turf" battles in favor of cooperation and collaboration. These reform reports provide motivation for taking some positive additional and public steps toward educational excellence at all levels, steps discussed for years and residing in the hopes and dreams of those who live their lives in the educational trenches of our schools and colleges. Now is the time to move toward educational quality—opportunity with excellence.

Former President Theodore Roosevelt once said that a great democracy must be progressive or it will soon cease to be either great or a democracy. That progressive search for excellence in education presses on in this country. There is relentless pressure to improve the quality of life, with education as the centerpiece of that process.

Although the reform reports have made important contributions, they exhibit some glaring omissions and blind spots which hold considerable significance for high schools and community, technical, and junior colleges. These deficiencies include: 1) failure to recognize that three out of four high-school students will probably not earn a baccalaureate degree; 2) sparsity of discussion about how to make winners out of ordinary students; 3) little emphasis on continuity of learning; 4) limited attention given to the great range of individual differences among the school population, particularly the one out of four students who does not complete the high-school program; 5) lack of participation by community, technical, and junior college personnel in these discussions despite the fact that fifty-five percent of all entering freshmen begin their college careers in one of these colleges.

This book addresses these issues and offers a major proposal to increase high-school/community college program cooperation and coordination. No attempt has been made to be inclusive or to discuss aspects of the reform reports that have been covered extensively elsewhere. In particular, no attempt has been made to assess the quality of teaching or teachers. We can only tip our hat in appreciation to those many talented and motivated individuals who keep the educational enterprise glued together. Rather, this study explores some not-so-obvious learning challenges facing the students of our high schools and community, technical, and junior colleges.

The leaders of high schools and colleges are urged to utilize this book to expand the dialogue where it is already in progress and to initiate the dialogue where it has yet to begin. It is hoped that this report will trigger hundreds of high-school/college roundtable discussions across the country.

Dale Parnell

Dale Parnell, *President*
American Association of
Community and Junior Colleges

ACKNOWLEDGEMENTS

MANY INDIVIDUALS have contributed to the development of this book. Special words of appreciation go to the American Association of Community and Junior Colleges Board of Directors and Executive Staff for inspiration and for allowing the author the time away from the office to complete the writing.

Several individuals reviewed manuscript drafts and made invaluable suggestions. This list includes: Judith Eaton, President of Community College of Philadelphia and Chair of the AACJC Board of Directors; Harold McAninch, President of the College of DuPage and Past Chair of the AACJC Board of Directors; Bernard Luskin, Executive Vice President of AACJC; Warren Bryan Martin, Scholar in Residence, Carnegie Foundation for the Advancement of Teaching; Thomas A. Shannon, Executive Director of the National School Boards Association; William Kendrick, Superintendent of the Salem, Oregon Public Schools; Sue Shields, Vice Principal of Sprague High School in Salem, Oregon; Scott Thomson, Executive Director of the National Association of Secondary School Principals; Arthur Cohen, President of the Center for the Study of Community Colleges; Florence Brawer, Research Director of the Center for the Study of Community Colleges.

Special thanks to Chancellor Jan LeCroy of the Dallas County Community College District and to his assistant, Nancy Armes. They gave this project a major push at a strategic time. Nancy Armes aided immensely in helping to formulate several of the difficult issues.

I am grateful to Valarie Brooks, who translated the writing into manuscript form and to Shirley Moyer, who helped manage the project. James Gollattscheck, Vice President for Communications for AACJC, has contributed much to the editing and publishing of this work.

I extend much appreciation to Barbara Shapiro, who helped edit the book, for her unflagging care and understanding. My appreciation is extended as well to Richard Rabil for his fine art work and to Diane Eisenberg for coordinating the book's editorial and artistic services. A special word of appreciation is also expressed to a long-suffering companion, Beverly Parnell. She provided inspiration when needed and patience in abundance.

Finally, thanks to the Shell Oil Foundation for financial support in the development of the book.

Dale Parnell

Chapter I

Some Dilemmas in Defining Excellence

More and more young people emerge from high school ready neither for college nor for work. This predicament becomes more acute as the knowledge base continues its rapid expansion, the number of traditional jobs shrink, and new jobs demand greater sophistication and preparation.

National Commission on Excellence in Education in *A Nation at Risk: The Imperative for Educational Reform*

A recent *Parade Magazine* article proclaimed the twenty best high schools in the country. The major criterion for the selection of these excellent schools was the percentage of high-school graduates going on to a four-year college or university and a baccalaureate degree. A review of this list of highly rated high schools reveals a great deal more about the socio-economic level of the student body than it does about the quality of teaching and learning going on in the classrooms. It also underlines the value given education by the families of these high-school students.

I recall my own experience as a young high-school principal in the 1950's in a large school representing a predominantly blue-collar population. Our rival across the river was situated near a large university and served a white-collar, university-oriented community. When the merit-scholars program was first inaugurated, there was great consternation when our high school had only one merit-scholarship winner and the high school across the river had ten. The media became interested and questions began to fly. Why couldn't our high school do as well? What was wrong with our high school? What were we going to do to improve our program? This invidious comparing of schools is still going on today, and my rejoinder of thirty years ago is still applicable:

There are many kinds of excellence, and the merit-scholarship program measures only one kind. We are not interested in measuring academic excellence by comparison of school to school. The socioeconomic differences are just too great. But we are interested in individual goals and individual progress. You see, we take our students one at a time, as individuals, rather than as a homogeneous group. Our faculty work hard to help individuals become merit-scholarship winners, but they work equally hard to help all students become good citizens, wise consumers, energetic wage earners, healthy individuals, supportive family members, and most

3

important, effective life-long learners. Our definition of excellence revolves around student progress in learning. We are proud of our academically talented students, but we are also proud of our students with other talents.

Most of us develop our opinions based on pictures in the head rather than on real facts. Unfortunately, the pictures in the head about excellence in education are based primarily on the notion that there is only one kind of talent and that all students are, or should be, headed for a college-prep/baccalaureate-degree program. The facts simply do not support such a view. The 1980 census reveals that seventeen percent of the American population twenty-five years of age and older hold a baccalaureate degree. *Even given a dramatic growth of baccalaureate-degree holders during this decade, at least three out of four of our students in the public schools are unlikely to achieve a baccalaureate degree.*

The Dilemma of Defining Excellence

The educational community is not alone in forming unrealistic images of excellence and imposing them on the American people. Madison Avenue has developed an advertising image of excellence based upon a thin, attractive, white family, confident and happy in its meticulously landscaped and spacious suburban home. Each morning, after a breakfast which provides fiber and builds bodies twelve ways, two children, perfectly groomed, emerge from a model kitchen and skip off to the neighborhood school, as meticulously landscaped and spacious as the family home. Presumably, within the allotted time they will be graduated. Then, with little or no effort, they will continue their education at the university whose pennants are already mounted on their artfully decorated bedroom walls.

Faced with such an artificial image of excellence, one can understand the chagrin and frustration of the ordinary student who has never entered such a world and of the local school-board member who, during a school-board meeting, jumped to his feet and informed his colleagues, with tongue in cheek: "I am so disgusted with our schools. Why, do you know that half of our students are below average?"

The television and movie image of excellence portrays fun and games as the standard way of life and celebrates the anti-hero. The multi-millionaire athlete or movie star or rock star with live-in boyfriend or girlfriend becomes the standard role model for our young people. John Belushi, Cyndi Lauper, Eddie Murphy, or Farrah Fawcett has a much stronger influence upon values than do teachers or sometimes even parents. Reading, writing, and arithmetic run a slow third to the more dramatic skills of Indiana Jones and the Beverly Hills Cop.

The news image of excellence stresses form over substance. The "photo opportunity" is more important than the message. How someone looks is far more important than what he or she says. In recent years the media have criticized the White House on this score, but they perpetuate the pattern themselves. Recently I was invited to a White House news conference on adult literacy. Former Secretary of Education Terrel Bell and President Reagan were to make an important announcement about a bold new national program to reduce adult illiteracy. The room was filled with reporters and photographers. President Reagan bounded into the room with his usual exuberance, wearing a new hearing aid in public for the first time. The photographers immediately began to take pictures of the President and his new hearing aid. After some preliminary statements about the new program had been made by the former Secretary and the President, the first question from the reporters was, "Mr. President, how long have you been wearing your hearing aid?" Adult literacy received scant attention from the media that day, but pictures of the President and his new hearing aid were published across the country.

In some institutions of higher education the definition of excellence begins and ends with the admissions process. Who gets in? Excellence will be more or less automatic if the entrance-screening process has been thorough enough in sorting and screening the academically talented from the not-so-talented. There is nothing inherently wrong with tough admissions standards as long as we do not allow college-entrance requirements to be viewed as the only key to excellence in a universal education system.

The comprehensive high school and the comprehensive community college work on the basis of a not-so-visible or dramatic

5

definition of excellence. They seek the development of a highly diverse potential in all students. Certainly these schools and colleges want a well-prepared entering student. However, there are many kinds of talents and many kinds of excellence. These institutions focus on progress in learning and in value added: where was the student upon entry and did he or she make progress?

Is the College-Prep/Baccalaureate Degree the Only Road to Excellence in Education?

One of our human failings is to assume that most people think and act as we do. Many in the field of education suffer from this malady. They have experienced the baccalaureate-degree program and therefore expect everyone to have a similar experience. Educational policy formation has become the monopoly of college and university graduates who appear to believe that academic excellence must be described primarily in terms of the kinds of education which they experienced. *The great debate about excellence in education is closer to a monologue of the one-sided opinions of well-meaning individuals and groups who have little contact with non-baccalaureate-degree America.* Isn't it time for community, technical, and junior college leaders to join in the debate alongside their university and public-school colleagues?

As an example, the College Board has been working for several years on an Educational EQuality Project and has issued an excellent publication entitled *Academic Preparation for College*. This report proposes to synthesize the judgments of several hundred teachers from a cross section of schools and colleges about what constitutes the learning students must bring from high school to have a fair chance to succeed in a baccalaureate-degree program. However, comparatively few community, technical, or junior college personnel were involved in this effort, and little attention was given to the host of ordinary students needing some post-secondary education and training, although not necessarily a baccalaureate degree.

A college-prep/baccalaureate-degree program is certainly the road to excellence for many individuals, and our schools and community colleges must help these students prepare for this direction in life better than ever before. Indeed, community colleges are actively pursuing programs to encourage and motivate more community college students to press on to the baccalaureate degree. But we must constantly remind ourselves that the majority of our population will never earn a baccalaureate degree. What about the ordinary student? What can we offer him or her? This student also wants and needs an excellent education, but one that is applicable to his or her talents and future. Are we creating the educational crisis of the 1990's by continuing to insist that one kind of educational program be applicable to all students?

K. Patricia Cross, professor at the Harvard Graduate School of Education, offers a pungent observation on this subject:

> In the final analysis, the task of the excellent teacher is to stimulate "apparently ordinary" people to unusual effort. What do the reports on school reform have to contribute to that goal? In the first place, there is surprisingly little attention given to "ordinary people" in the school reform reports. There is the clear implication that the rising tide of mediocrity is made up of embarrassing numbers of ordinary people. Teachers' colleges are advised to select better candidates, colleges are encouraged to raise admissions standards, and the federal government is urged to offer scholarships to attract top high-school graduates into teaching. There is not a lot said in the education reports about how to stimulate unusual effort on the part of the ordinary people that we seem to be faced with in the schools and in most colleges . . . The tough problem is not in identifying winners; it is in making winners out of ordinary people. That, after all, is the overwhelming purpose of education. Yet historically, in most of the periods emphasizing excellence, education has reverted to selecting winners rather than creating them. (Cross 1984)

At a recent international conference on higher education David Moore, Principal of Nelson and Colne College in Lancashire, England, commenting on the British educational system, said, "Our schools in England are designed to make the majority of our people feel like failures." (Moore 1984) After reading the recent plethora of recommendations about improving American education one might conclude that excellence in American education can only be achieved by making a majority of students feel like failures, unable to cope with modern life. *Anything less than a college-prep/baccalaureate-degree program is viewed as somehow second-rate.* Few of these national studies provide a workable solution to the problem outlined twenty years ago by John W. Gardner:

> The importance of education is not limited to the higher orders of talent. A complex society is dependent every hour of every day upon the capacity of its people at every level to read and write, to make difficult judgments, and to act in the light of extensive information . . . When there isn't a many-leveled base of trained talent on which to build, modern social and economic developments are simply impossible. And if that base were to disappear suddenly in any complex society, the whole intricate interlocking mechanism would grind to a halt. (Gardner [1961] 1984)

Can the Ordinary Student Experience Excellence in Education?

We tend to live somewhere between our hopes and our fears. It is possible for our age to move closer to our universal-education hopes and dreams rather than to our fears? Can we provide an excellent universal-education system for all our citizens in their diversity? The United States has come closer than any other culture to achieving this high goal, but the enterprise must still be called an experiment. *We have yet to demonstrate that we really know how to provide a universal education for all people.* In particular, how can we help ordinary students feel like winners? We must face up to the dilemma of achieving excellence in a universal-education system, particularly for the ordinary student.

The American education system moves along slowly, somewhat like the little English "puffer" tugboats moving through the fog in an age prior to that of depth-finders and radar. Usually a young boy was hired to sit on the bow of the puffer, tossing pebbles first to the right and then to the left to be sure the boat was in the middle of the channel. As our present education system moves through the fog, there seem to be an unusually large number of pebbles being tossed right and left to keep our educational "puffer" from running aground. We have not yet invented the kind of radar that will make it easier to determine where we are in our universal-education effort, nor have we developed a common understanding of the word "excellence" or related that common understanding to the educational enterprise.

The National Commission on Excellence in Education states our present dilemma in this straightforward way: "More and more young people emerge from high school ready neither for college nor for work. This predicament becomes more acute as the knowledge base continues its rapid expansion, the number of traditional jobs shrinks, and new jobs demand greater sophistication and preparation." (Gardner et al. 1983)

What is disappointing in the content of the major education reform reports is their lack of emphasis on learning incentives and learner motivation. Meanwhile, almost half the Hispanic high-school students in the country drop out before graduating from high school. This is more than double the rate of black students and three times the rate of white students. Forty percent of the Hispanic drop-outs never complete the tenth grade. The National Commission on Secondary Schooling for Hispanics states: ". . . the high drop-out rate is a failure of the education system which has not met the aspirations and special needs of its growing Hispanic population." (*Washington Post* 1985) The Commission blames curricula that fail to address the vocational needs of students, the lack of adequate counseling and support services, low expectations, and the strength of the work ethic among Hispanic men.

The Dilemma of Meeting Individual Differences

The current national thrashing around, the report upon report on how to improve the schools and colleges, are symptoms of the still-experimental nature of the American education enterprise. The sheer diversity of individuals attending the schools is awesome. The varieties of student aspirations and abilities, of socio-economic and cultural backgrounds, require multiple approaches in program and in the teaching/learning process.

9

One of the pressing dilemmas for educators is how to meet the great range of individual differences among students while seeking the best in all people, whether rich or poor, able or disabled, destined for the university, community college, apprenticeship, military, or a specific job, including homemaking. *To that end, we must learn to ignore, indeed to laugh at, the assumption that a baccalaureate degree is the sole road to excellence, respect, and dignity for all people.* Social and educational status cannot be confused with equality of opportunity and individual achievement, regardless of the field of study. It will be a sad day indeed if the "excellence movement" becomes a cover for a retreat from equity and opportunity concerns. As stated by the Commission on Pre-College Education in Mathematics, Science and Technology, "Excellence and elitism are not synonymous." (Coleman et al. 1983) Clearly, American education requires a new definition of excellence in education, a definition that will hold meaning for *all* students.

For educators at all levels, it is a time when the varieties of excellence we aspire to achieve in our universal education system must match to a sufficient degree the sheer diversity of our students. Trend analysts, forecasters, policymakers, strategic planners—all are finding dramatic ways to underscore what we have already begun to understand in a visceral way. The information age, sped by technological advance, presents a richer, more complex reality in which an increasing number of human beings want and need more of life and work. In that context, education is facing some imposing challenges, particularly in helping the ordinary student develop the competencies and the proficiencies required to successfully, even joyfully, cope with the dilemmas of a rapidly changing world.

The Dilemma of Change

We are living in the time of the parenthesis, the time between eras, John Naisbitt tells us. "It is a time of ambiguity, of change, and questioning, a time electric with possibilities, when a single model for achievement will always be limiting, a time when those able to anticipate the new era will be a quantum leap ahead of those who hold on to the past." (Naisbitt, *Megatrends*, 1984)

10

Frankly, some new models are required for education based upon individual student needs and the needs of a rapidly changing society.

If a higher quality of work life is to become a reality for millions of Americans, perhaps the most fundamental emerging truth is that higher and more comprehensive skills must be developed, particularly by the middle two quartiles of the work force. More sophisticated manual as well as conceptual skills will be in demand, and this worker cohort will be pushed consistently to handle a broader range of work requirements. Tasks once reserved for baccalaureate-degree or advanced-degree performers will be assumed by those with fewer years of education and training, and all workers will find it essential to learn throughout their careers in order to remain useful. Not only do we anticipate that these demands will surface in the future, but we know what human resources will be available to meet these demands: all who will be part of the work force in the year 2000 are alive today. Thus we can extrapolate much from the age, sex, ethnic, and regional mixes about the kind of individual working at any level.

It just may be easier to create an information-age society than to maintain one. Since we know less about job replacement than job placement, more about training than retraining, and more about excellence in some aspects of education than in others, we must learn quickly new skills of program coordination and continuity in order to provide greater structure and substance in the learning process for *all* individuals.

We have been told that in the future there will be a greater number of individuals in our society working at low-skill jobs, i.e., as clerks, custodians, waiters. But sheer volume does not give an accurate picture of job replacements or of future employment-skill needs, especially of the new career-competency requirements created by an information society. Certainly, there have been and will continue to be a large number of low-skill, low-pay jobs requiring minimal skills. It is likely there will always be a more-than-adequate supply of individuals possessing only those minimal skills. But that tells only part of the story. "Occupational Employment Projections" lists the twenty fastest-growing occupations from 1988 through 1995 (Figure 1). None can be classified as low-skill, and only two or three obviously require a baccalaureate degree for entry. The remainder of these fast-growth jobs are occupations for which some postsecondary education and training, but not necessarily a baccalaureate degree, are preferred or required.

As a further example, the electronic industry is moving close to becoming a $400 billion business, and it is predicted that within a year or two seventy-five percent of all its jobs will involve computers in some capacity. The American Electronic

Figure 1

Twenty Fastest Growing Occupations, 1982–95

Occupation	Percent growth in employment
Computer service technicians	96.8
Legal assistants	94.3
Computer systems analysts	85.3
Computer programmers	76.9
Computer operators	75.8
Office machine repairers	71.7
Physical therapy assistants	67.8
Electrical engineers	65.3
Civil engineering technicians	63.9
Peripheral EDP equipment operators	63.5
Insurance clerks, medical	62.2
Electrical and electronic technicians	60.7
Occupational therapists	59.8
Surveyor helpers	58.6
Credit clerks, banking and insurance	54.1
Physical therapists	53.6
Employment interviewers	52.5
Mechanical engineers	52.1
Mechanical engineering technicians	51.6
Compression and injection mold machine operators, plastics	50.3

Source: U.S. Department of Labor, "Employment Projections for 1995," Bureau of Labor Statistics, U.S. Government Printing Office, March 1984.

Association report entitled "Technical Employment Projections 1983-87" indicates that the electronic industry will need a sixty-percent increase in technicians by 1987. That means 115,000 new electronic technicians will be needed within two years, in addition to older-worker replacements.

The shift from an agricultural society to an industrial society took about one hundred years. But the current movement from an industrial society to an information society is taking place so rapidly there is little time for reaction. The information society is a hard, here-and-now, economic reality. Between 6,000 and 7,000 scientific articles are written each day. Technical information is doubling about every five years.

Our society will always need custodians and waiters, with their own sense of excellence, but it is more myth than reality that technology will diminish the need for workers possessing a middle range of technical skills and a better educational background than ever before. That need will grow dramatically.

Over the last decade we have been entering a "product life-cycle" as we have embraced the information age. This initial phase has been pushed along by the more advanced skills of scientists, engineers, and top-level management. However, with growth and maturity comes the commercialization of technology. Economic history tells us that the volume of need for a mid-range of workers (which this report designates as technicians) will grow rapidly as various technologies move out of the development phase into the production phase of the product life-cycle. These are the individuals who will help us maintain and adapt to our technology-driven information age. Figures 1 and 2 reveal that the employment growth is most pronounced in the managerial, technical, sales and precision production, craft and repair categories of work.

The Dilemma of Technology

John Naisbitt traces the occupational history of the United States from farmer to laborer to clerk, from rural to blue-collar to white-collar America. He invites us to speculate about the new workers who will characterize the predominance of our work force as we move past the parenthesis into a new era.

13

Obviously, what is required is a worker who has obtained an excellent education that has enabled him or her to develop a cluster of skills that reflects many of the critical trends encapsulated here, a worker who is broadly educated and whose responsibilities may span several work areas. What is required for many occupations in the future is a broad technician rather than a high technician, if by that term we are describing an employee who:

- understands the basic principles of technology in an information age saturated with the use of technology.
- connects practice and theory in the work world.
- identifies problems and then analyzes, tests, and trouble shoots to find solutions.
- integrates the interests of complementary work areas.
- works independently with a network of individuals much of the time, under the general supervision of a highly skilled, frequently more narrowly specialized professional.
- works willingly and well with his/her hands as well as with the brain.
- has mastered a basic-skills package that includes a core of competence in math, science, computer science, and communications.
- is liberally educated to function competently as a citizen, a consumer, a family member, and a neighbor.
- has developed the proficiencies to be a life-long learner.

In its recent report examining the quality of learning under its purview, the National Science Board Commission on Pre-College Education in Mathematics, Science and Technology warned that technology must be considered a new entity by educators, not an extension of science and mathematics: "The main implication for education of the saturation of society with technology is that understanding technology becomes a primary concern . . . It is not true that understanding science and mathematics conveys an equal understanding of technology." (Coleman et al. 1983)

Other analysts warn that if technology becomes an isolated content domain, our society will create more problems than it will solve. Their conclusions about the effect of technology on science and math apply to the broad spectrum of career interests in this nation. Technology can compartmentalize us more or make us more responsive. It can create greater understanding and involvement within the work force, or it can isolate us one from the other.

It is estimated that pure high-technology jobs will account for only five to six percent of all U.S. jobs by 1990. It should be

Figure 2
1983 and 1984 Comparisons
Occupational Status of the Employed

Occupation	One Year Growth Civilian Employed	
	August 1983	*August 1984*
Total, 16 years and over	**103,167**	**106,694**
Managerial and professional specialty	**23,044**	**24,460**
Executive, administrative, and managerial	10,814	11,789
Professional specialty	12,230	12,671
Technical, sales and administrative support	**31,840**	**32,924**
Technicians and related support	3,091	3,175
Sales occupations	12,140	12,891
Administrative support, including clerical	16,608	16,858
Precision production, craft, and repair	**12,794**	**13,641**
Mechanics and repairers	4,230	4,477
Construction trades	4,602	5,023
Other precision production, craft and repair	3,963	4,141
Operators, fabricators, and laborers	**16,498**	**17,193**
Machine operators, assemblers, and inspectors	7,905	8,105
Transportation and material-moving occupations	4,198	4,480
Handlers, equipment cleaners, helpers, and laborers	4,396	4,608
Construction laborers	674	732
Other handlers, equipment cleaners, helpers, laborers	3,721	3,875
Service occupations	**14,510**	**14,291**
Private household	1,015	1,000
Protective service	1,827	1,757
Service, except private household and protective	11,667	11,535
Farming, forestry, and fishing	**4,481**	**4,185**

Source: U.S. Department of Labor, "Employment Projections for 1995," Bureau of Labor Statistics, U.S. Government Printing Office, March 1984.

pointed out that agriculture was probably the first high-technology industry, making two blades of grass grow where only one grew before; there is nothing particularly new about technology. What is important to note is the impact of technology upon nearly all forms of work. On this point John Naisbitt comments: "The industrial economy rested upon the automobile, but not all of us worked directly with automobiles. Nonetheless, our lives were significantly altered by them. Similarly, the information economy rests on the computer, but not all of us will work directly with computers. Our lives and our jobs, however, will certainly be changed because of them." (Naisbitt, *The Year Ahead*, 1984)

Broad technology and not high technology will characterize the main influence on the development of our nation's work force in the future. We predict here that the occupational history of this country will chronicle the steps from farmer to laborer to clerk to *technician*. Technicians, that is broad-technology technicians, will act as the force that holds together the thousands of potentially isolated elements in our work world. They will be the individuals who not only understand underlying principles, but also have the ability to apply what they have learned. These are the generalists with specific practical skills to address typical day-to-day challenges. The development of this kind of worker will require some new programs and approaches to education. In particular, some new thinking about vocational education will be required.

A Dilemma for the 1990's

Are we creating the crisis of the 1990's by indiscriminately imposing baccalaureate-degree program standards upon high-school graduation requirements? Is this the answer to improving the high-school education of the ordinary student? It may motivate some students, but surely it will discourage others. When seventy-five percent or more of our high-school graduates do not complete the baccalaureate degree and twenty-five percent of those who begin high school do not even finish, one must question the validity of the current educational program for the great mass of individuals in the middle quartiles of the typical high-school student body. What kind of educational program will meet the needs of these three out of four students? Can these students experience excellence? Will requiring more theoretical physics or theoretical math meet their needs and abilities? Of course not, but they certainly need more than "bachelor living," "arts and crafts," and hobby-type courses. Some fundamental shifts must be made in school and college programs if the needs of *all* students are to be met and the universal education enterprise is to be moved up the road a few more miles. Comprehensive high schools and comprehensive community, technical, and junior colleges *must be* concerned with improving the educational program and performance of the ordinary student *along with* the baccalaureate-degree-bound student. It is not an either/or proposition.

Chapter II

Some Persistent Tensions in Achieving Excellence

Excellence and elitism are not synonymous.

National Science Board Commission on Pre-College Education in Mathematics, Science and Technology

I would put the subject of school drop-outs first. It is absolutely astounding to me that so many intelligent people could look for so long at American schools and say so little about this problem.

Harold Howe
Harvard Graduate School of Education

The cultivation of excellence in education must be accomplished in a social and educational milieu of perplexing divisions and tensions. Any attempt to "fix" American education cannot be accomplished in isolation. It must be accompanied by an examination of related issues and the possible impact of these issues on other parts of society.

There are three great social tensions in our contemporary society that must be recognized as part of any discussion about excellence in education. They are a *technological tension*, an *educational tension*, and a *socio-economic tension*. How we define excellence in education will determine whether we can reduce these tensions. Indeed, examination of these tensions may provide us with some key indicators as to the health of our democratic society and of the educational system that supports that society.

A Technological Tension

The first of the social tensions is *technological*. Our society grows technically and scientifically more sophisticated, yet continues to produce an increasing number of individuals who are uneducated, unskilled, and unable to cope with these technological changes. Is the pool of the uneducated and unskilled growing or is it shrinking? No one knows for sure. We do estimate that some twenty-three million individuals cannot read, write, or compute at a functional level. We do know there are still seven to eight million individuals unemployed and another three to four million working part-time but looking for full-time work. We also know that the nature of work is shifting from blue-collar labor to white-collar clerical to gray-collar technical. We also know that a single inoculation of education for the young is no longer sufficient for a lifetime.

21

Much has been made of the need to increase the number of engineers and other baccalaureate-degree personnel to meet the demands of a high-technology society. But little attention has been given to preparing the mid-level technicians that keep the planes flying, the cars repaired, the hospitals operating, the buildings constructed, the computers serviced, the laws enforced, and generally keep our country running. As an example, the health industry is booming, requiring individuals with a strong technical education background: the nurses, health technologists, and technicians skilled in the use of diagnostic and therapeutic equipment.

In fact, a labor shortage, which this writer predicted four years ago, is now upon us. The labor force is growing slowly—from 110 million to 130 million between now and 1995: an increase of twenty million workers. At the same time, we are seeing jobs created by small and medium-sized businesses increasing at an unprecedented rate. In 1983 some four million new jobs were created, with close to another four million added in 1984. If new jobs continue to be created at even half this rate while the population continues to age and older workers leave the work force, a critical worker shortage is inevitable. Add to this picture the movement toward downskilling. Tasks once reserved for baccalaureate-degree performers are being relegated to technicians and those with fewer years of education and training. This is an almost automatic by-product of the commercialization of technology and the evolution of the product life-cycle.

Recently, much attention has been directed toward helping individuals at the other end of the scale. In general, federal and state job-training programs have been designed for the hard-core unemployed. The results have been discouraging, particularly where rather sophisticated skills have been required.

The tensions between high unemployment and skilled-worker shortages will become greater unless some very specific steps are taken. The Index of Help Wanted Advertising offers evidence of the mismatch between the needs of the workplace and the skills of American workers. This index is a seasonally adjusted measure based on the number of help-wanted advertisements printed in the classified-advertising section of leading newspapers. While unemployment remained at 7.6 percent during May of both 1980 and 1981, the help-wanted index increased from 112 to 118. Simply put, more job openings were reported, but unemployment did not go down. Since then, unemployment has gone up significantly and is now leveled out at about the 7.5 percent figure. *It is a tragedy that tremendous opportunities exist on the one hand while sizable unemployment remains on the other.* Eric Hoffer has observed that young people are warned not to waste their time but are being brought up to waste their lives. The waste of human resources creates tremendous tensions in our society.

The shortage of skilled workers is also documented by the U.S. Department of Labor in a publication entitled *The Forecasting of Manpower Requirements.* This publication projects a shortage of adequately trained personnel in certain professional and technical occupations. The House Committee on Armed Services asserts that labor shortages penetrate deeply into the lower tiers of the industrial base. Currently there are shortages in the number of skilled production workers, machinists, electronic technicians, tool and die makers, test technicians, optical personnel, and skilled assemblers.

A number of factors make it evident that the shortage of skilled workers will only grow worse in the years to come. The work force in this country is aging, meaning that the proportion of older to younger workers is increasing. The average age of tool and die makers is about fifty-nine years. The number of people aged sixty-five and over is growing about twice as fast as is the population of the nation as a whole.

The time is ripe for some new thinking about the technological tension and related job training. *For example, why not develop a national program which gives a pat on the back and active help to members of the underclass who have already taken the first steps toward lifting themselves out of their environment?* The most cost-effective job-training program today may be one that focuses on upward mobility. Why not identify those proven workers in dead-end jobs and offer them education and training to meet the needs of new jobs requiring new and more sophisticated skills? This would be a win-win situation. The employee would move up, the employer would gain a proven worker, and an entry-level job would be opened for an unskilled or less skilled worker.

An Educational Tension

Most of the national education study reports offer their own definitions of quality, but few comment at any length upon access to education or upon creating more opportunity. *One of the increasing tensions is educational. Can we have quality and equality in education? The obvious answer is that a democratic society must have both.*

The national groups issuing these reports have not been particularly interested in the continuing increase in the number of high-school drop-outs. A smaller share of American youth is graduating from high school today than a decade ago. The percentage of entering high-school students that graduate has dropped from 77.2 percent (a 22.8 percent drop-out rate) in 1977 to 72.8 percent (a 27.2 percent drop-out rate) in 1982. This means there has been a nearly five-percent increase in high-school drop-outs over the last decade. (Grant and Eden 1982)

In 1979, eighty percent of white nineteen-year-olds were high-school graduates, while sixty-four percent of blacks and sixty percent of Hispanic nineteen-year-olds held high-school diplomas. Furthermore, the ethnic and racial composition of young America is shifting. Slightly more than twenty-five percent of white Americans are under eighteen years of age as well as fifty percent of the Hispanics and thirty-three percent of blacks. While minorities make up about ten percent of the general American population, they average twenty-seven percent of the school population.

We seem to have a *bifurcated* view of our high schools. Some see the high school as a sorting system separating the academically talented from the not-so-talented. Others see the high school as the "holding pen" for young people, keeping them off the job market until they have grown up. *Not enough people see the high school as a human-resource development laboratory, a place in which to prevent human waste.* The debate rages on. Can there be quality and equality in the American school system?

24

The National Commission on Excellence addresses this question:

> We do *not* believe that a public commitment to excellence and educational reform must be made at the expense of a strong public commitment to the equitable treatment of our diverse population. The twin goals of equity and high-quality schooling have profound and practical meaning for our economy and society, and we cannot permit one to yield to the other either in principle or in practice. To do so would deny young people their chance to learn and live according to their aspirations and abilities. It also would lead to a generalized accommodation to mediocrity in our society on the one hand or the creation of an undemocratic elitism on the other. (Gardner et al. 1983)

The most serious educational tension is a self-induced program fragmentation that focuses primarily on either an academic or a vocational education track. For those students who do not fit comfortably into one or the other, we offer an unfocused general-education track leading to nowhere.

Let us talk a bit about tracking in high school. Academic, general, and vocational tracks tend to set up unnecessary and arbitrary division and conflicts. Conflicting opinion exists among secondary-school educators as to whether tracking even exists in most high schools. Coleman and colleagues found that in eighty percent of the cases teachers and principals disagreed about tracking, teachers acknowledging and principals denying its presence. (Adelman 1983) In the National Center for Education Statistics data bases, students reported tracking in their high schools. Fetters found a significant amount of agreement between students and administration on the existence of track placement, with seventy-eight percent agreement on academic track placement. (Fetters 1975)

Whether we agree or not that academic, vocational, and general education tracking is operating in high schools, a majority of teachers and students perceive a tracking system. In fact, few would disagree that the college-prep/baccalaureate-degree track has been highly visible throughout the history of the American high school.

25

Tracking patterns spring from the traditional division of the arts into the liberal and fine arts and the practical arts. Although the American education system is derived from an elitist philosophy, the populist tradition blossomed early, as more and more individuals saw education as their pathway into the economic mainstream of American life. In 1892, 500,000 students went to high school; in 1983-84 nearly sixteen million were enrolled. The classical liberal and fine arts education no longer seemed uniformly appropriate. As a consequence, and I believe an unintentional consequence, rigid boundaries were drawn between the liberal and practical arts, although these boundaries create an unnecessary tension. The liberal and fine arts bring meaning to life in many ways and liberate the individual by developing the creative and spiritual senses. The practical arts bring a focus to life that helps individuals move from dependence to independence; few experiences are more liberating than developing vocational competence. All are needed for ensuring educational excellence. Clearly, the liberal, fine, and practical arts must move closer together. If for no other reason, the demands of the information age will require the easing of this needless educational tension. But in easing the tension we must not forget the needs of an increasing volume of students. These are the students who are resisting the outmoded academic and vocational labels and who are permitted, as a result, to fall without plan or purpose into something called "general education."

We talk about the wage earner, the citizen, the family member, but not enough attention is given to the life-long learner in our society. If there is one thing in which the schools and colleges should excel, it is in helping the individual to develop the competencies to function in this role. What are the competencies that must be developed to be an effective life-long learner? Here is a skeletal list: reading speed and comprehension skills, analytical skills, memory-training skills, problem-solving skills, decision-making skills, synthesizing skills, human-relations skills, computational skills, and more recently, computer skills.

Under our current educational practices, if an individual has not developed these competencies to a certain level by the end of the eighth grade or so, he or she has been doomed forever to educational purgatory. How many barriers have been constructed for adults who need to improve their "learner" skills? Many of us would like to improve our reading speed or our analytical skills or our memory skills or our intergroup human-relations skills and communications skills. Where do we turn? Where is the home in the high-school and college curriculum for individuals to develop these specific competencies to become more effective life-long learners? Many community colleges have established developmental education programs or college-preparatory departments to address these needs. However, they have done so over the protests of legislators, academicians, and those who have a more exalted "picture in the head" about education. In fact, the college-credit and related financing systems often actually mitigate against meeting the student at the point of his or her "learner" needs.

Peter Drucker indicates that the greatest single barrier to improving the productivity of our nation is the consistent breakdown in intergroup and interpersonal communications. Employers indicate consistently that their greatest concern is with employees who fail in the human-relations and intergroup-relations categories. More employees are dismissed because they cannot get along with others than for any other reason. Where is the home in the school or college curriculum to address this need?

Employers designate the ability to learn as the essential hallmark of the successful employee. Yet, in most educational arenas little direct time is spent on the learner skills of problem solving, synthesis, analysis, and critical thinking. *Helping individuals develop the competencies to be effective life-long learners should be the top priority of any educational institution.*

There are other educational tensions that tend to bog us down. Here are a few examples:

Upper-level high-school science and math continue to be too abstract and theoretical for perhaps two-thirds of the student body who desperately require a better and more practical education in math, science, and communication skills. The Morrill Act of 1862 was developed to connect the practical *and* the liberal arts for an agrarian society. Yet land-grant colleges and most postsecondary institutions have still not resolved what "practical" means, nor have they managed a happy marriage of the two. The definitions and use of tools and applied knowledge are pointedly absent from the education of most secondary-school young people, although the practical expressions such applied knowledge represents are essential to the quality of work we produce in a technological world.

Learning has leaped the boundaries of schools and colleges. More and more learning opportunities are offered through employers or community-based organizations. As an example, some 475,000 individuals received their high-school diploma in 1983 via the GED testing program. An estimated 950,000 individuals across the nation earned college credits via extra-institutional learning in 1983. An increasing number are earning college credits for learning acquired in the military, on the job, through independent study and televised learning. Yet most schools and colleges seem oblivious to this phenomenon.

A broad-based systems approach to technical training will discourage career obsolescence, we are told. But in practice the new career courses most often added reflect an increasing specificity of emphasis, and we continue to prepare individuals for specific jobs rather than for careers.

Finally, perhaps a key tension for some open-door community colleges is that they have side-stepped the need to work closely with high schools and to state clearly their own preparation expectations for high-school students. If they are to have the best chance for success in a community college, high-school students must have a clear sense of what it will take to succeed. Yet, most young people hold only vague notions of what adequate preparation for a community, technical, or junior college experience means. *In the great haste to separate themselves from high schools, too many community colleges have weakened or nearly severed the high-school/community college connection.*

A Socio-Economic Tension

The third great tension is *socio-economic* in origin. There is a continuing and widening gap between the "haves" and the "have-nots" in our society. Syndicated columnist William Raspberry comments on this issue:

> The 1964 Civil Rights Act, and other legislation spawned by that movement, ended official racism, and meritorious blacks were quick to take advantage. But solving that problem introduced another—in many ways, tougher—problem. To a significant degree, America today really does treat blacks as individuals. It looks at education test scores, economics and other evidences of individual merit. A 1980's Ralph Bunche could live, work, go to school or eat a meal at the place of his choosing.
>
> The principal victims of racial disparity today are the non-Ralph Bunches: the unskilled, uneducated, unambitious, economically crippled underclass whose problems, though they might have had their own origins in racism, would not be solved by an end of racism.
>
> This, though many of us have difficulty seeing it, is a different set of problems whose solution is beyond the reach of a mass movement. Groups can be granted the full range of opportunities, but only individuals can take advantage of them.
>
> The pressing question now is how to help the underclass—and clearly they will need help, private and public—to translate theoretical opportunity into actual improvement of their status. (Raspberry 1984)

An increasing stratification seems to be taking place along economic, educational, employment, and ethnic lines. Statistics show a recent increase in the number of individuals and families in the lower-income strata and below the poverty line. There also appears to be a steadily increasing gap between low- and middle-income families and upper-income families. Janet L. Norwood, Commissioner of the Bureau of Labor Statistics, reports a drop in the February 1985 unemployment rate from 6.4 percent to 6.2 percent for whites but an increase from 14.9 percent to 16.3 percent for blacks. (*Washington Post* 1985)

When we consider the situation of the "haves" and "have-nots" in our society, four startling statistics emerge:

- Two out of three adults who currently meet the federal definition of poverty are women and more than half the poverty families are maintained by single women.

Figure 3

The Haves and Have-Nots

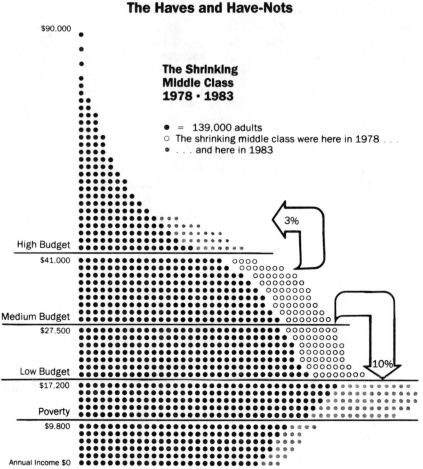

The Shrinking
Middle Class
1978 · 1983

● = 139,000 adults
○ The shrinking middle class were here in 1978 . . .
● . . . and here in 1983

$90,000

High Budget
$41,000

Medium Budget
$27,500

Low Budget
$17,200

Poverty
$9,800

Annual Income $0

3%

10%

This chart is adapted from the wall-size poster "Social Stratification in the United States," recently published by Social Graphics, a Baltimore company that prepares posters on controversial issues. Stephen Rose, the economist who created the chart, explains that between 1978 and 1983 approximately 13 percent of the middle portion of the middle class (as defined by the Bureau of Labor Statistics) disappeared. Of this 13 percent, one quarter rose into the upper-middle-class category, and three quarters descended into the lower middle class. Furthermore, the number of people below the poverty line increased 3 percent. This downward shift represents a significant change in the nature of the American social fabric.

Source: Stephen Rose, "Social Stratification in the U.S." (Harper's, 1984), 27.

30

- Seventy percent of all AFDC (Aid to Families with Dependent Children) recipients are children.
- 3.1 million children, or 3,000 a day, have fallen into poverty since 1979. This is a thirty-one-percent increase in the number of poverty children over a five-year period.
- There has been a fifty-two-percent increase over the past eight years in working women with infants under one year of age. (American Enterprise Institute for Public Policy Research 1983)

The politically conservative observe these facts and aver that competition and choice are the keys to helping the poor. All ships rise with the tide: major emphasis must be placed upon overall economic growth if the poor are to be helped. Along with an improved national economic program, local and state efforts should be mounted to strengthen the capabilities of individuals and families to meet their needs.

The politically liberal look at the statistics and call for a national full-employment policy with jobs at the heart of the anti-poverty strategy. All barriers to working should be removed and some type of federally funded job-guarantee program should be developed. National, state, and local efforts must be exerted to help young mothers and young children. This includes emphasis on prenatal and infant health care, child-care programs for working mothers, and federally financed help in improving reading and math of poor children.

While the political forces continue to debate and disagree, the pool of the poor continues to grow. The poor continue to be caught in a cycle of unemployment, loss of self-esteem, and poverty. Unfortunately, the vast majority of the poor are women with children. This has prompted the National Council on Economic Opportunity to say: "All other things being equal, if the proportion of the poor in female-householder families were to continue to increase at the same rate it did from 1967 to 1978, the poverty population would be composed solely of women and their children before the year 2000." (Ehrenreich and Stallard 1982)

Working women who are poor and supporting a family (particularly young children) must be classified as some of the most

31

heroic individuals in our country. Day in and day out they survive at standards just above welfare level. They can afford rent, minimal child care, food, and some kind of transportation, and that is about all. They pray daily that their children will remain healthy. For the single woman with children there are few provisions and scant encouragement to seek additional education and training to help move into the economic mainstream. Indeed, public policy seems to deny low-income women many opportunities for upward mobility. Community, technical, and junior colleges deserve plaudits in this area. Most of these institutions have made significant efforts to design programs that reach out to the displaced homemaker and single female parent who must work. Individuals who work in these programs can tell some of America's most dramatic and heart-lifting stories. One of these, related by Don Newbury, President of Western Texas College, is symbolic of thousands:

Mary Lou Moreno, a thirty-four-year-old cosmetology student at Western Texas College, was so determined to get to class on a fifteen-degree morning in the winter of 1983 that she set out to hitchhike the thirty-five-mile distance after her car failed to start. She had already missed several hours of training because of car trouble, and she knew she could be dropped from the program if she continued to be absent. There is no public transportation between Snyder, where the college is located, and Rotan, where Moreno lives with her five children. So she began to walk and, after being given lifts by three passing motorists, arrived two hours after classes had begun. Her eventful day came to a climax in late afternoon when a classmate sent her a basket of flowers to say what an inspiration she was to her fellow students. That day also just happened to be her birthday. Her dedication and commitment eventually paid off: in June she passed the state cosmetology exam and is now working as a cosmetologist.

Why is it that it is only when we discuss governmental aid to poor people that a subsidy becomes a dole? We don't use the word "dole" when we discuss subsidies for farmers, or Pell Grants for college students, or stipends for veterans, or tax breaks for corporations, or tax shelters for the wealthy. *Ironically, even the rhetoric we use shoots an arrow at the self-esteem of the poor.*

Rather than view the poor as untapped human resources, we tend to view them as problems.

Many other implications must be considered in reviewing the socio-economic tensions between the "haves" and the "have-nots," but the major question to consider is what education and training can do to help. We have never really developed a national human-resource-development strategy in this country, particularly for non-baccalaureate-degree individuals. No discussion of excellence in education in a universal education system can be complete without considering the plight of all members of society and the tensions that motivate or inhibit them. *It is time to value our human resources as much as, if not more than, we value our natural resources of oil and gas and metals.*

Chapter III

Some Barriers to Excellence

During what now seems like a golden age of American education, there were two clear, specialized tracks. There was a good academic track for the university-bound students and a good vocational track for work-bound students. The "general" track—which led to limbo—was small. But the Excellence Commission notes that the number of students on this general track, this track leading to nowhere, has increased from one in eight to nearly one in two. And that, more than anything, is the center of the problem.

Marvin Feldman, President
New York Fashion Institute of Technology

The academic and vocational desert of American education is the high-school general-education program. Too many young people are receiving an unfocused general education which relates to nothing, leads to nothing, and prepares for nothing. It certainly does little to promote continuity in learning or to build personal confidence and self-esteem. *Unfocused learning remains one of the prime barriers to achieving excellence for a host of high-school students.*

In recent years there has been such a significant movement of high-school students from both the academic track and the vocational track into the unfocused general-education track that this program has now become dominant in most high schools. In a recent study high-school seniors were asked to describe their present high-school program. The students could mark "academic or college preparatory," "general," or any of the seven "vocational" areas. The following table summarizes the findings:

Figure 4
High School Comparative Track Identification

	1969	1975–81
Academic Track	48.8%	36.4%
General Track	12.0%	42.5%
Vocational Track	25.6%	19.0%
Missing Cases	13.6%	2.1%

These general-education students spend over forty percent of their high-school effort outside the traditional academic courses, compared with thirty percent for the academic-track students. The academic courses for these students often carry titles such as General Science, General Social Studies, General Math, Remedial English. Nevertheless, more and more of these same students aspire to college and regard themselves as well prepared for college attendance. (Astin 1982, Wagenaar 1981)

The high-school curriculum of the general-track student can best be described as a combination of general, remedial, and personal/hobby courses. Even though general-track students take fifteen percent of their high-school credits in vocational-education courses, there is little evidence of any kind of focus or concentration. Nearly half the high-school time of the general-education student is spent in personal-service and development courses such as physical education, arts and crafts, home economics, and work experience.

Is it any mystery that general-track high-school students are unfocused in their learning, more alienated toward school, and have a significantly higher drop-out rate? (Echternacht 1976) Is it any wonder that these young people experience a significant increase in self-esteem two or three years *after* they leave high school? Students going into the armed forces are among those with the lowest self-esteem in high school but the highest self-esteem two years later. ("Two Years after High School," n.d.) *Having a goal, meeting a challenge, and being pushed to one's limit are what build self-esteem.*

The "High School and Beyond" survey asked 1980 seniors to evaluate various aspects of their schools. The general-education students rated their school experience as less satisfactory than did academic or vocational-track students and were least satisfied with the quality of academic instruction and teacher interest in students.

One of the most powerful and instructive statistics about the general-education track is that 63.5 percent of the high-school drop-outs indicate they were in the general-education track at the time they left high school. Only 6.7 percent of the drop-outs came from the academic track, while 29.8 percent came from the vocational program. ("Two Years after High School," n.d.)

The present system of pot luck in the schoolhouse, where students take a little of this and a little of that, provides young people with too many loopholes, too little reality therapy, too many excuses for failing to learn and failing to develop basic

Figure 5

Percentage of 1980 Seniors Agreeing with Various Statements About High School Education or Practice, by Curriculum and School Type

Statements	All Seniors	Curriculum Academic	Curriculum General	Curriculum Vocational	Type of School Public	Type of School Private
Schools should have placed more emphasis on vocational and technical program	70	57	75	81	55	63
Schools should have placed more emphasis on basic academic subjects	67	67	67	65	72	48
School provided me with counseling that will help me continue my education	64	67	58	61	66	69
School did not offer enough practical work experience	59	52	63	60	50	65
School provided me with counseling that will help find employment	44	35	43	57	36	30

Source: Samuel S. Peng et al, **High School and Beyond: A Capsule Description of High School Students** (U.S. Department of Education, National Center for Education Statistics, 1981), 16.

Figure 6

Percentage of 1980 High School Seniors Rating Various School Characteristics as "Good" or as "Excellent," by Curriculum and School Type

School Characteristics	All Seniors	Curriculum Academic	Curriculum General	Curriculum Vocational	Type of School Public	Type of School Private
Reputation in the community	68	77	64	64	73	90
Library facilities	67	66	67	71	68	60
Quality of academic instruction	63	75	55	60	73	85
Condition of buildings School spirit	62	69	60	60	67	76
Teacher interest in students	56	66	48	50	62	82

Source: Peng, 13.

39

Figure 7

Major Curriculum Components, Percentage of Credits Generated, by Track

| | Academic | | General | | Vocational | |
	1969	1981	1969	1981	1969	1981
A. Traditional Academic						
Language Arts	21.0	19.6	21.2	19.4	20.2	18.1
Social Studies	15.9	14.9	18.8	15.3	16.5	14.0
Mathematics	14.0	13.4	10.2	10.4	10.4	9.2
Sciences	12.6	13.2	10.2	9.3	9.4	7.9
Foreign Languages	11.5	7.7	3.3	3.2	3.1	2.2
Other Humanities	1.5	1.4	2.3	1.8	1.5	1.4
Sub-Total (84 courses)	**76.5**	**70.2**	**66.0**	**59.4**	**60.8**	**52.8**
B. Vocational						
Business/Office	2.2	3.3	5.7	5.5	10.8	9.2
Industrial Arts	2.6	3.1	6.8	6.9	8.7	11.7
Other	0.7	1.2	2.2	3.0	3.2	3.9
Sub-Total (24 courses)	**5.5**	**7.6**	**14.7**	**15.4**	**22.7**	**24.8**
C. Physical and Health Education (3 courses)	**9.1**	**9.1**	**9.2**	**9.8**	**7.6**	**8.9**
D. Basic Personal Service						
Typing 1	2.4	2.6	2.5	2.9	2.9	2.9
Home Economics 1	0.5	0.6	0.8	1.2	0.9	1.3
Music Performance	3.1	4.3	2.2	3.1	1.5	1.9
Sub-Total (3 courses)	**6.0**	**7.5**	**5.5**	**7.2**	**5.3**	**6.1**
E. Personal Service, Hobbies, Remedial (12 courses)	**2.1**	**4.3**	**3.1**	**6.6**	**2.5**	**5.8**
F. Other (5 courses)	**0.8**	**1.3**	**1.5**	**1.5**	**1.2**	**1.6**
Total:	**100.0%**	**100.0%**	**100.0%**	**100.0%**	**100.0%**	**100.0%**

Source: Clifford Adelman, "Devaluation, Diffusion and the College Connection" (unpublished paper, March, 1983), Appendix F.

proficiencies. Unfocused learning remains one of the great barriers to excellence for far too many high-school students.

One of the important lessons yet to be learned by many educators is that the "why" of learning is more important than the "how." Nietzsche's words, "He who has a *why* to live for can bear with almost any *how*," apply to education. Those students who see no connectedness, no aim, no purpose to their education,

40

also often see no point in continuing in school. *We live best by living on our hopes rather than our fears, by looking to the future.* The student who sees no future for himself or herself will also not make much progress in education.

Victor Frankl illustrates this point through relating an experience in a World War II Nazi concentration camp: "... any attempt to restore a man's inner strength in the camp first had to succeed in showing him some future goal ... Whenever there was an opportunity for it one had to give a *why*—an aim—for their lives, in order to strengthen them to bear the terrible *how* of their existence." (Frankl 1963)

Educators have a heavy responsibility to help students see meaning in their educational program. Clear goals for the curricular course or program and clear goals for the individual student are absolutely essential to achieving excellence in education. Student goals will change from time to time, indeed should change, but those changes do not invalidate the need for short-range goals. We all shoot better when we can see the target. It is a great disservice to allow high-school or college students to wander aimlessly through the curriculum with few, if any, targets at which to shoot.

If students are to be motivated to learn, they must know why they are learning, how this learning connects with other learning, and where this learning relates to real life. If we want instructors to be motivated to teach, administrators motivated to lead, school-board members and college trustees motivated to develop wise policies, and the public motivated to support our schools and colleges, we must pay unrelenting attention to purposes. These purposes must be developed with such precision and with such clarity that all involved will be able to develop a sense of personal meaning and commitment.

Unfortunately, goal development and goal setting have never been driving forces in the educational enterprise. Discussion of goals has become the intellectual sauna bath of education. Individuals gain a rosy glow in discussing these high principles and purposes, but the impact soon wears off as the bracing cold of real life returns. The result is a lack of continuity, coherence, and connectedness in much of the educational program.

Some time ago I attended a college executive-staff meeting at which institutional and related program goals were being discussed. One of the administrators jumped up to leave in the middle of the meeting. When asked where he was going he said, "I must get back to work; I don't have time to talk about goals." He failed to see either the connection between his work and the goals of the college or the discussion of institutional or program goals as part of his work. Unfortunately, this attitude is not unusual among school and college staff members at any level of the operation.

Loss of Continuity in Learning

One of the disappointing aspects of the major reports on educational reform is the scant attention given to continuity in learning. It is amazing that some students learn as much as they do, given the tremendous gaps in the substance of their learning as a result of irregular class attendance.

There is a close correlation between poor attendance patterns and poor grades. In fact, irregular class attendance is an early signal of course failure and eventual dropping out of the school or college. High-school principals report that poor student attendance continues to remain one of the key problems affecting the quality of education in their schools. Yet, how much attention has been given this subject in the reform reports? The answer is not much.

In 1982, the National Center for Education Statistics asked 571 school districts, on behalf of the National Commission on Excellence, which policies or procedures were most important for improving academic achievement. Increased daily class attendance was listed by sixty-six percent of the sample and ninety percent of the urban school districts as the most important. School leaders estimate a tremendous loss of continuity in learning and consequent school failures through absenteeism. It is one of the consistent barriers to excellence.

It is a fairly safe bet that overall student achievement-test scores would improve dramatically in most schools if student-attendance patterns improved. On the skill-acquiring levels, continuity in learning is extremely important. If the student misses one or two basic steps, the next steps become increasingly difficult to negotiate. As a consequence, one out of three or more students is constantly endeavoring to catch up. It is sad that most of these students spend the rest of their lives attempting to catch up and never really do.

Fred Hechinger, long-time observer of the American educational scene, has commented on the loss of continuity in learning:

> We are not very good at continuity . . . as a result of that, American education during the past few decades has become a collection of disjointed parts that in the main fail to connect . . . The lack of continuity that plagues American education is something that all of education needs to address. Instead of connecting the separate levels, critics generally compound the spirit of separation by seeking scapegoats instead of remedies . . .
>
> If we want to reform the schools, two things are essential: continuity, all the way up the line; and understanding the "why" of every single course. Read Bruno Bettelheim on that. Whatever you teach, make the children understand why they are studying it. Don't tell them: "You'll need it later." Later doesn't exist. (Hechinger 1984)

There are other facets to the problem of continuity in learning. America is a mobile society, and that very mobility has contributed to a tremendous loss of continuity in learning. An estimated twenty to twenty-five percent of public-school students attend more than one school each year.

Schools by and large operate on the basis of local control and local autonomy. Consequently, the transient student rarely experiences the same curriculum in any two schools. Basically, the American school system still operates as a cottage industry. From school to school teachers approach the curriculum differently and use different textbooks. The student is thrown into a new and often strange environment with a new teacher or teachers, a different curriculum, and told to sink or swim. The teacher will do his or her best to help, but with thirty other students, or 150 in high schools, he or she has little time for individual attention. Insufficient attention has been given to the loss of learning continuity in a highly mobile society. It remains a significant barrier to achieving excellence in education.

Other gaps cause loss of continuity in learning. How about the gap between high schools and colleges? For some students this gap must seem like the Grand Canyon. A gap also exists between high-school and college faculty. Some of this distance can be attributed to structure, which inhibits communication. *High-school instructors talk with high-school instructors, community college instructors talk with community college instructors, and university instructors talk with university instructors. It is only by much effort that the educational communication lines are crossed.*

Unlike European systems, which operate with a central ministry of education, the American education system is highly decentralized. There are 14,140 independent school districts and 1,222 dependent school districts (subject to the fiscal control of county or city government) across America. Responsibility for the actual operation of the schools has been delegated by the various states to local school districts (excepting Hawaii, which has one state-wide school system).

There are 1,221 public and private two-year community, technical, and junior colleges, 1,992 public and private four-year colleges and universities, and an estimated 6,000 proprietary (private) technical schools. The private colleges operate in a largely autonomous manner. The public two- and four-year colleges operate under local boards of trustees or as a part of a state university system or as an independent state system operating one segment of colleges. In addition to that institutional fragmentation, many have observed that there is no organism on earth more autonomous than a professor in a major university.

As a consequence of this highly decentralized educational structure, communication among and between the various entities and personnel involved becomes exceedingly difficult. Special efforts, particularly at state levels, are required to improve communication among education and educators at all levels.

The Twelfth-Grade Throw-Away

For too many students in too many high schools the twelfth-grade experience doesn't amount to much. Many students arrive at that point in their high-school experience needing only two or three credits to graduate. As a consequence, the twelfth grade becomes a "goof-off" year, a phenomenon which has seemed to increase since the late 1960's. It should be noted that the move in nearly all states to increase graduation requirements should do much to correct this problem. Nevertheless, far too many high-school seniors are enrolled in unstructured and unfocused programs lacking in substance. Can excellence be cultivated and a first-rate education achieved when half or more of a high-school senior class do not see this as a very important year of learning for them? With so much to be learned and so many new skills to be developed, students must make better use of the twelfth grade.

Many leaders of technical education programs in community colleges are now observing that excellence in technical education cannot be achieved in two college years, given the current preparation level of the students entering these programs. Wouldn't it make educational as well as economic sense for schools and colleges to utilize the twelfth grade more wisely instead of extending the technical programs to three college years?

Individual Differences

If we are to become serious about meeting that great range of individual differences in comprehensive high schools and comprehensive community colleges, instead of permitting half our students to slip through the "general education" crack we must cultivate a goal-oriented educational-program diversity to match the diversity of the student body and levels of preparedness. But we cannot hope to develop such an appropriate educational diversity unless we recognize various forms of excellence. We must reject the idea that excellence can be found only in certain university-oriented programs or in preparing for certain professions.

John Gardner has distilled some of our best thoughts on the varieties of excellence:

Though we must make enormous concessions to individual differences in aptitude, we may properly expect that every form of education be such as to stretch the individual to the utmost of his potentialities. And we must expect each student to strive for excellence in terms of the kind of excellence that is within his reach. Here again we must recognize that there may be excellence or shoddiness in every line of human endeavor. We must learn to honor excellence (indeed to demand it) in every socially accepted human activity, however humble the activity, and to scorn shoddiness, however exalted the activity. As I said in another connection: An excellent plumber is infinitely more admirable than an incompetent philosopher. The society which scorns excellence in plumbing because plumbing is a humble activity and tolerates shoddiness in philosophy because it is an exalted activity will have neither good plumbing nor good philosophy. Neither its pipes nor its theories will hold water. (Gardner 1961)

The greatest single challenge facing instructors in elementary schools, secondary schools, and to a significant degree in comprehensive community colleges is how to meet the great range of individual differences in every classroom. In desperation schools have labeled students bluebirds, robins, and meadowlarks, or advanced, terminal, and remedial, and are still missing the mark. Consider the following: A thirty-five-year-old reading at the fourth-grade level (math skills arc probably at the same level of competency) wishes to take training to prepare for a job. This is what he or she faces:

- On the average, it takes fifty hours of intensive one-on-one tutoring to raise an adult one grade level in reading.
- It usually takes the average adult 150 hours of adult basic-education classroom time to advance one grade level in reading or math.

How many thirty-five-year-olds will or can commit this amount of time *just to get ready* for job training? A shocking quotation from a 1979 Ford Foundation study tells the story: ". . . all current literacy efforts combined are reaching less than four percent of those in need."

What can be done? Some high schools and community colleges are developing a less labor-intensive alternative teaching-learning approach using low-cost microcomputers as the core, along with other communications technology and with tutors. Research data from one producer of basic-skills software claim that children on the average will rise one grade level in reading in twenty hours on a computer and rise one grade level in math in twenty-five hours on a computer. The development of the microcomputer, the video cassette recorder, and similar technological breakthroughs hold much promise for helping instructors meet the teaching challenges of individual differences. The VCR in particular is becoming common in homes and classrooms. The school and college library of the future will experience increasing pressure to accommodate video learning tapes and discs.

Can these technologies be used to teach basic skills to adults? Central Piedmont Community College in Charlotte, North Carolina, is gathering data to answer this question through its ABLE (Adult Basic Literacy Education) project, which combines microcomputers, VCRs, audio tapes, sound slide programs, and television.

A news article describing the ABLE project in personal terms recently appeared in *The Charlotte Observer*:

Miracles are not confined to the Bible nor Thanksgiving to a single day of the year. Come to Freedom Mall Shopping Center and observe a man whose mind is blind to the printed word be made to see. Willie Loyd is about to shuck the chains of functional illiteracy, free at last to embrace a world denied him all his life. Willie is learning to read.

He takes his seat before a small cubicle in the shopping center store space converted into a Central Piedmont Community College classroom. Willie slips on a pair of blue headphones. He turns on his Apple computer and the message from the cassette through the headphones tells him to punch certain computer keys. He does so.

What Central Piedmont is doing is to combine in a single program the best of technology and literacy teaching skills that have developed recently as well as long ago. Frank Laubach pioneered a method to teach adults to read and write, beginning in 1930 in the Philippines. But where it may take fifty hours of individualized tutoring to move a student one elementary grade level in reading, computer-assisted learning can do it in about twenty hours.

47

Images About Learning Become Barriers to Excellence

One of the tremendous problems we must overcome in addressing individual differences in education is failing to separate the images from the realities. These inaccurate pictures in the head about learning, as related to individual differences, continue to present imposing barriers to achieving excellence in education. The following images must be separated from the realities before significant progress can be made in the movement toward excellence.

Images	Reality
1. Students all learn at approximately the same rate of speed.	1. There are vast individual differences among students of any age in speed of learning and comprehension of knowledge.
2. All students learn the basic skills by completion of the elementary grades.	2. Development of basic skills must be placed upon a continuum of learning with students arriving at different points at different times. Excellence in education requires breaking the lockstep of arbitrary time requirements for learning.
3. Students who fail to achieve in school either do not want to learn or are unable to learn.	3. Research suggests that given adequate time for learning, and favorable learning conditions, ninety-five percent of students can achieve mastery of any basic skill.

4. The traditional textbook and lecture method of instruction is the most effective method of teaching for most students.

4. Some students learn rapidly by one method of instruction and more slowly under a different approach. However, after fifteen years of experimentation and experience in more than 3,000 schools, mastery teaching-learning appears consistently more effective than traditional instruction.

5. Real excellence can only be found among those students and programs related to pursuance of a baccalaureate degree.

5. Every high-school and college program must develop standards of excellence. Excellence is just as important to the aircraft technician as to the engineer. The notion of excellence must be extended to every course and each student.

Chapter IV

Career Goals and Educational Excellence

The high school should help all students move with confidence from school to work and further education. Today, we track students into programs for those who "think" and those who "work," when, in fact, life for all of us is a blend of both. Looking to the year 2000, we conclude that, for most students, twelve years of schooling will be insufficient. Today's graduates will change jobs several times. New skills will be required, new citizenship obligations will be confronted. Of necessity, education will be lifelong.

Ernest L. Boyer, *High School: A Report on Secondary Education in America*

S idney P. Marland Jr., the United States Commissioner of Education, stood before several thousand secondary-school principals in Houston, Texas, on January 23, 1971, and kicked off a bold new movement in American education by saying:

Most of you are secondary school administrators. You, like me, have been preoccupied most of the time with college entrance expectations. Vocational-technical education teachers and administrators have been either scorned or condemned and we have been silent.

There is illogic here as well as a massive injustice. How can we blame vocational educators for the hundreds of thousands of pitifully incapable boys and girls who leave our high schools each year when the truth is that the vast majority of these youngsters have never seen the inside of a vocational classroom? They are the unfortunate inmates, in most instances, of a curriculum that is neither fish nor fowl, neither vocational nor truly academic. We call it general education. I suggest we get rid of it . . .

. . . The first attitude that we should change, I suggest, is our own. We must purge ourselves of academic snobbery. For education's most serious failing is its self-induced, voluntary fragmentation, the strong tendency of education's several parts to separate from one another, to divide the entire enterprise against itself. The most grievous example of these intramural class distinctions is, of course, the false dichotomy between things academic and things vocational. As a first step, I suggest we dispose of the term vocational education, and adopt the term career education. Every young person in school belongs in that category at some point, whether engaged in preparing to be a surgeon, a bricklayer, a mother, or a secretary.

What has happened to career education over these past fourteen years? The phrase has almost been eliminated from the educational vocabulary. In fact, "career education" appears about ready

53

to join the long list of oxymorons circulated as jokes, like "military intelligence," "legal brief," and "congressional action."

Was career education a bad idea? What has been the residual impact of the career education movement? No one knows for sure what happened to career education, but it is fairly safe to say that much of the salutary information developed about career education has been lost in the current rhetoric about academic excellence.

Some Images of Career Education

The career-education movement has nearly foundered because of a lack of definition and a fuzzy image. *What is the picture that pops into your head when you hear the phrase "career education"?*

Let us examine some current images of career education. Depending upon orientation and background, one can summarize these images under six or seven categories. First, the general public still has what can be called the "old car" image. *For many people career education is a group of boys gathered around an old car.* Even many teachers have inherited this image. Far too many individuals see career education as something applying primarily to boys working with their hands and as purely vocational.

Next, some educators have what can be called the "dumb/smart" image. As far as they are concerned, career education is for all the "dumb kids" and so-called academic education is for all the "smart" students. Somehow we have not yet eliminated the words "dumb" and "smart" from our educational vocabularies. Much has been discovered over the past twenty years about learning and the process of intellectual growth. Benjamin Bloom, one of the leading educational researchers in this country, recently made the following comment: "We have learned that individual differences in learning are differences in rates of learning, not in basic ability or capability. With appropriate teaching methods as many as ninety percent of students have learned, in time, up to the level of the top ten percent in earlier groups."

The 1973 National Teacher of the Year, Jack Ensworth of Bend,

Oregon, has stated this concept in another way: "If only the beautiful birds sang, the forests would be quiet indeed."

Regardless of the research and despite our rhetoric about the uniqueness of each individual, many people still advocate that "academic" means advanced and is for the "smart" students and that career education is for the "dumb" students.

Here is an interesting illustration of the way in which the dumb/smart image makes an impact on the curriculum. About twice as many jobs require welding as a background skill and experience as jobs which require chemistry. Yet nearly every high school has a chemistry laboratory and chemistry courses, while relatively few high schools have welding labs or offer welding courses. Why? Many school boards and school administrators indicate they can't afford a welding lab, but they can afford the expensive chemistry lab which does not have the potential of serving nearly as many students as does the welding lab. This illustration does not denigrate chemistry, but only illustrates our tendency to put our money on what the "picture in our heads" envisions as important.

A third fallacious image of career education can be called the "foot-stool and end-table" image. Have we made enough end tables and foot stools in our school wood-working shops for a spell? If there is any single great weakness in the career education movement, it is in the middle grades, seven through ten. Home-making teachers and industrial arts teachers must be challenged to lead the way in devising opportunities for boys and girls to explore all career families or clusters of occupations in the laboratories, in the subject-matter classrooms, and in the communities. If we limit our definition of career education to "fooling around" in the shop, making another foot stool, we have missed the mark. Perhaps now is the time to suggest that what we have known as industrial arts be considered prevocational rather than vocational training.

Another image can be called the "playtime" image. This writer recalls visiting the classroom of a second-grade teacher who was proud of the work she had been doing in "career education." The students had spent much of the school year building a scale-model barn. Although it may have provided a certain amount of learning experience, the school's principal described the project as a disorganized game. He said that although the students had enjoyed the project, tests revealed they had not improved their skills in reading, writing, or computing. They probably didn't learn very much about farming as a career, either. At this point, one can only recall the misunderstanding and misapplications of the theories of John Dewey and other "progressive" educators. *If we allow career education to become another form of recess, it will continue to evaporate as have some other fine notions in education.* Career education should bring more meaning to the curriculum, not less. A barn-building project could be used to improve basic skills, while at the same time informing young-sters about some of the careers associated with agriculture and construction.

Principals, like other people, often operate on the basis of pictures in their heads, and their images of career education can also be inaccurate. Some administrators have developed what might be called the "dumping ground" image, which is closely related to the "dumb/smart" image. *In their high schools, one could well retitle the woodworking shop classes Dumping Ground I for the sophomores, Dumping Ground II for the juniors, and Dumping Ground III for the seniors.* The wood shop often becomes a place where students are dumped when school counselors and administrators do not know what else to do with them. Often, the vocational teacher is good at handling students with behav-ioral problems and so "shop" is where the behavioral problems are dumped. An obvious question must be asked: How many of these behavioral problems are created because the student sees no purpose, no meaning, in his or her academic program? Does that student see a relationship between what he or she needs to meet the challenges of real life and his or her schooling experi-ences?

Certain legislators have another image of career education. This is the "we can't afford it" image. At a legislative hearing I can recall a state senator, who also happened to be a junior-high-school teacher, talking about the cost of career education. Lean-ing back in his chair, he said, "We can't afford career education. Why, did you know that you could build fourteen or fifteen regular high schools for what it costs to build one vocational high school?" This image errs in two ways. First, career education and vocational education should not be confused. The separate vocational-high-school idea limits the notion of career education to specific job training for certain jobs. Second, the senator's cost estimate is only an image in his head. A vocational high school such as he envisions would have gold-plated door knobs and marble halls.

True, some specific job-training classrooms do cost more to equip than do English classrooms, but many of them do not. As an example, speech is one of the communication skills required for many careers, e.g., law enforcement, nursing, sales, teaching, the ministry. Yet, the speech class is not viewed as a part of the career-education program in most schools. Plainly, the erroneous image in the head must be replaced with a more accurate picture of what career education is about.

Plato Over Aristotle

American education over the years has favored Plato's ideas of "classical education" over the more practical ideas of Aristotle. In fact, an important body of leaders in this country today holds that anything called "vocational education" has no place in the school curriculum; that the term "education" refers only to the development of the intellectual proficiencies and knowledge dissemination. Socrates followed this line of logic: "This is the only education which, upon our view, deserves the name; that other sort of training which aims at the acquisition of wealth or bodily strength, or mere cleverness apart from intelligence or justice, is mean and illiberal, and is not worthy to be called education at all."

Scholar and long-time observer of the American educational scene, Keith Goldhammer rebuts this position:

> The establishment of a public-school system in the United States based upon the Platonic intellectual tradition has tended toward an elitist conception of its functions, has emphasized its selective characteristics, and has at least partially abrogated its responsibilities for the seventy-five to eighty percent of its students who by native ability, interest, and aspiration are identifiable with the

57

practical affairs of our culture rather than inclined toward the more abstract and conceptual activities of the academic disciplines . . .

That which is needed in today's world is neither a new brand of academicism nor a new style of vocationalism, but a fusion of the two. The emerging conception which may obliterate the false dichotomy between the academic and the vocational is that of careers education. (Goldhammer and Taylor 1972)

Black intellectuals Booker T. Washington and W. E. B. DuBois spent much of their lives debating the issue of the academic versus the practical. DuBois was interested primarily in educating gifted black youth, believing that if well educated, the gifted would educate and lead the masses. Washington emphasized education for the masses, self-employment, and the necessity for black young people to work with both their heads and their hands. He believed that "The Intellectuals," as he called them, understood theories but were not knowledgeable enough in practical matters to become well-educated artisans, businessmen, and property owners.

Although in later years DuBois admitted that Washington was right, it was too late to turn the tide; DuBois' position had gained the ascendancy. As an example, in Washington, D.C., a city that is seventy percent black, vocational education has generally received the cold shoulder. The District Board of Education allotted less than four percent of its 1984 budget to the vocational high schools, which enroll over ten percent of the high-school students. There is the lingering feeling that vocational education represents something inferior. (Press 1984)

When Washington Technical Institute was merged with the University of the District of Columbia, it didn't take long for many of the two-year technician-education programs to be phased out as unfitting for a university curriculum. *Isn't it amazing that we honor tennis as something worthy of college credit, but self-defense for a law enforcement officer as unworthy, or welding as art as worthy of college credit, but welding as an occupation as unworthy?*

If, on the other hand, we believe it should be the primary purpose of education to help each student become a fully competent, self-motivating, self-fulfilling member of our society, then it is time to dust off the literature and to redirect the old career-education discussions toward a careers-*education orientation.* The evidence indicates that life roles in one form or another remain the central and dominating force in the lives of most human beings, and the requirements of these various life roles should be the beginning points for any discussion of educational goals. *One of the reasons dissatisfaction is often expressed about modern schools is that we have failed to match in any systematic way the goals of schooling with the life-role needs of individuals living in our modern society.*

Information Rich—Experience Poor

James S. Coleman has called the society of seventy years ago "information poor but experience rich." (Coleman 1972) People received most of their information from books or from neighbors, but they were involved in all kinds of experiences. Usually children were given responsibilities or chores from which they learned practical skills and gained experience.

Today we live in a different society, an information-rich but experience-poor society. In fact, children acquire so much information from television that many suffer from too much data. They are not emotionally equipped to assimilate or interpret all they see and hear without the personal experience that provides realistic perspective. They see a president shot and brutal scenes of wartime combat before their eyes before they have seen a dead rabbit or suffered the loss of a pet dog. When they enter the classroom they are confronted with even more information, often as ambiguous as and generally less interesting than that on television.

How, then, can schools provide experiences that will enable students to relate information to the real-life roles that constitute a part of living for all but a few of the most handicapped? That is the question that careers education can answer. It is the primary purpose of careers education to help connect information and knowledge with real-life experiences. Young people of today and tomorrow need an information-rich, experience-rich educational program.

Maslow's Theory of Basic Human Needs

Abraham Maslow's theory of basic human needs provides instructive insight into understanding the purpose of careers education. Maslow contends that the human being is motivated by several basic needs. These needs are intrinsic and generic and are organized into a need hierarchy of relative potency. Throughout his life a person is always desiring something and is satisfied completely for only brief periods. As each desire is satisfied it is replaced by another.

Most individuals in American society have partially satisfied many basic needs while still maintaining, unsatisfied, others that motivate and drive them. Maslow found that individuals who satisfy their basic needs are healthier, happier, and more effective, while those whose needs are frustrated develop psychopathological symptoms.

The most powerful and basic need is for survival, both physiological and emotional. Maslow indicates that once the survival needs are satisfied to a degree, safety needs emerge. Any good teacher of young children knows that the child needs a secure world. When security and a degree of consistency are absent, the child becomes anxious. With a preponderance of survival and safety needs met, the needs for love and belonging emerge.

The fourth level of need revolves around at least two kinds of esteem needs: self-esteem and respect from others. Self-esteem needs include feelings of competence, confidence, achievement, and independence.

Finally, after adequate satisfaction of the love and esteem needs, the need for self-actualization generally emerges. This highest level of need stems from that constant human drive to explore the human potential and nurture that potential into all it can become. (Maslow 1954)

What does a hierarchy of needs have to do with the goals and purposes of schooling? The first purpose of the great American dream called "universal schooling" is to meet each individual at the point of his or her need. Unfortunately, schools and colleges too often meet students at the point of institutional rather than student need. One must look at the basic needs of human beings to gain an understanding of student need. If the first level of need is survival, does it make sense to force every student to sit through the self-actualizing experiences of Shakespeare and Homer and ignore his or her survival needs? This is not to intimate that literature is unimportant; however, if schools and colleges are to meet students at the point of their greatest need, the motivational aspects of the graduated scale of need must be recognized.

Human needs are motivational in nature and must be met, at least partially, in rank order. American schools and colleges often aim for the self-actualizing and higher-level needs while ignoring the lower-level needs, particularly self-esteem needs. What competencies are required to build self-esteem? What kinds of competencies are required to cope successfully with life as a citizen, wage earner, consumer, and learner? Careers education can help develop these competencies so that students will see reality and meaning in their education. When schooling focuses on the real-life career roles of individuals and the competencies required to cope with those careers and roles, we will see a positive educational change for the neglected majority of our students.

By giving young people a variety of opportunities for real-life experiences, we will solve several problems indirectly. Traditionally, we have tried to attack emotional, racial, ethical/moral, and cultural problems by telling people what to do—telling them to be moral, for example. But schooling must be more than telling. It must provide opportunities for students to experience and cope with real situations.

Through real-life experiences, the high-school student of tomorrow can begin to feel more confident about himself or herself. He or she can feel tolerant toward others by developing the skills required for coping with real life. Schooling will provide the student with a healthy atmosphere as rich in experiences as in information. Thus, schooling of the 1990's and beyond will provide students with esteem-building experiences to enable them to act as independent, contributing citizens in the remaining decade of the twentieth century and beyond.

Careers education affords students opportunities to meet the basic human needs of survival, security, belonging, self-esteem, and self-actualization. Through this curriculum, the schooling experience will provide genuine involvement in learning because real-life needs will determine the purposes and priorities of secondary-school education.

Needed: Some Real-Life Therapy

The school curriculum has not kept in step with the times and with the real-life needs of a changing society. The needs have changed, but the schools and the school curriculum have not. *We still operate information-rich but experience-poor schools.*

The competencies required to cope with real-life roles and their relationship to the school curriculum are the crucial issues facing the schools today. These issues are interrelated, and the measure by which they are made compatible will largely determine the significance of all schooling activity. The fact that schools are busy and teachers are skilled does not necessarily mean that the schools are accomplishing the right things. Two questions must be asked of modern schools: Which real-life needs are you meeting? How well are you meeting these identified needs? These questions must be posed continually.

It is common for students to know more about the Eskimos of Alaska and the Incas of Peru than about their own city council, the property taxation system, the justice system, or even voting in elections. The percentage of young people eighteen to twenty-four participating in our elections has dropped about twenty percent over the last decade (see Figure 8). Most young people haven't the foggiest idea who levies the taxes that support their own schools and how or why they are levied. As we examine the changes in our society over the past seventy-five years, we find that in our highly urbanized society some citizenship problems are apparent that were not apparent when one could ride one's horse to the county seat. For example, we don't talk much in our schools about citizenship on our streets and highways, yet over 40,000 people are killed annually in traffic accidents.

During the tenure of this writer as superintendent of public instruction in Oregon, an excellent curriculum guide on local and state governments was published by the State Department of Education. I was visiting a U. S. history and civics teacher one day and asked, "How do you like the curriculum guide on local governments?"

"Oh, I'm not using it. I'm too busy teaching about the federal government. I just don't have time to get into state or local government."

Our curricula and textbooks are filled with emphasis on the federal government. *Our students must know about the U.S. Constitution and the Bill of Rights, but we just don't seem to have time to do much with local and state governments, the*

Figure 8

Percent of 18 to 24 Year Olds Reported Having Voted, 1962–1982

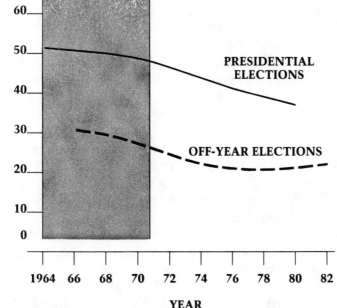

NOTE: The shaded area is the period prior to passage of the constitutional amendment which lowered the national voting age to 18. From 1964 to 1970, the minimum voting age was 21 in 46 states and the District of Columbia, 20 in Hawaii, 19 in Alaska, and 18 in Georgia and Kentucky. Thus, for the 1964–1970 period, the graph shows the proportion of 18–24-year-old voters from among those who were eligible under varying state laws.

Source: Current Population Reports, Series P-20, no. 397, "Voting & Registration in the Election of November 1984" (advance report), U.S. Bureau of Census, 1985.

governments closest to the people. There is a tremendous lack of congruence between what we emphasize in schools and the competencies required to cope with modern life, even in the area of citizenship. *In short, real life feels mighty uncomfortable in the school and college environment.*

Life Roles

A life role is usually described as that which an individual performs throughout his or her life. The role is defined by the expectations that an individual and others have for it as well as by certain ideal norms that society in general attaches to it. The "life careers" roles with which all of us are simultaneously involved include the roles of individual (being myself, being an "I"), life-long learner, family member, producer, consumer, and citizen. The role of individual includes participation in avocational pursuits and being aware of and committed to aesthetic, moral, health, and spiritual values.

The question then becomes, how does schooling relate to those life roles? Successful performance in life roles requires more than knowledge, yet for some educators in the Platonic tradition, the main business of education is knowledge dissemination. Students should be told about their life careers or roles and should receive information relating to those roles. But that is not the same as recognizing that they are living those roles every day, in fact are experiencing life roles with or without the kind of schooling that will help enable them to achieve a measure of success and fulfillment—yes, even survival—in those roles.

It is the objective of careers education to help individuals develop the proficiencies to be able to cope successfully with whatever may be thrown at them in their various life roles. The reason careers education must be revisited is clear enough: the educational establishment itself just may be finally convinced that the ideas of Plato will not suffice in a universal contemporary educational program. Any honest look at our schools reveals that they are failing to meet a majority of the real-life needs of a majority of students. *Far too many of our current educational practices and requirements are based not only upon the philosophy of Plato, but also upon the needs of a society of seventy or eighty years ago.* Young people have indeed outgrown our present-day schools.

We can see seven great strands running through the school curriculum: these are the competencies related to the life roles of learner, citizen, consumer, wage earner, individual, leisure-time pursuer, and family member. The first four strands comprise the primary areas of accountability for the schools. The latter three are shared with the home and other agencies and represent the secondary areas of accountability for education. Schools share accountability with the home, the church, television, and other governmental agencies to help young people develop the competencies to function effectively as family members, self-renewing individuals, and leisure-time pursuers. The schematic representation that follows (Figure 9) is suggested as a careers-education paradigm around which to structure the school curriculum.

Let's Call It Careers Education

What is the correct image of careers education and how can present inaccurate images be changed? When the goals and objectives of any organization or enterprise are fuzzy, the actions of the organization tend to take on the same fuzziness. American education suffers from a "fuzzy goals" syndrome. We can't ask educators to be held accountable unless we first spell out what they are to be held to account for.

Let's look at a notion or two that might bring a degree of clarity. *First, let us define careers education as that delivery system which helps students develop the competencies required to function in the real-life roles of learner, wage earner, citizen, consumer, family member, leisure-time pursuer, and individual.* Thinking in terms of the competencies required to function effectively in life roles is one way of removing the fuzziness from the goals of schooling. Schools could begin by diagnosing student needs as related to these life roles. It is the hope of this writer that every state legislature would also join in the goal-setting task. *The point of access for policymakers into the teaching/ learning process should be determining what should be accomplished by schooling, not how it should be accomplished.*

65

Figure 9

Careers-Education Paradigm

Career Role Competencies

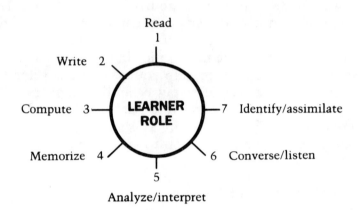

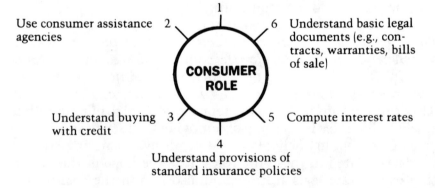

Figure 9 continued

Career Role Competencles

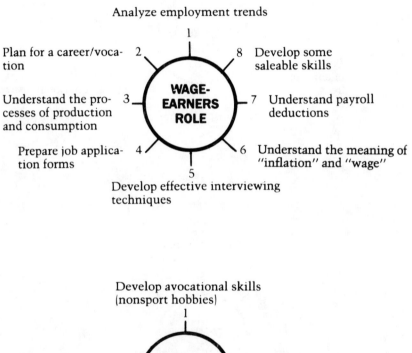

Analyze employment trends

1

Plan for a career/voca- 2   8 Develop some
tion   saleable skills

WAGE-EARNERS ROLE

Understand the pro- 3   7 Understand payroll
cesses of production   deductions
and consumption

Prepare job applica- 4   6 Understand the meaning of
tion forms   "inflation" and "wage"

5

Develop effective interviewing
techniques

Develop avocational skills
(nonsport hobbies)

1

LEISURE-TIME ROLE

Create something 2   4 Develop recreational
                               skills (sports)

3

Enhance aesthetic appreciation

Figure 9 continued

Career Role Competencies

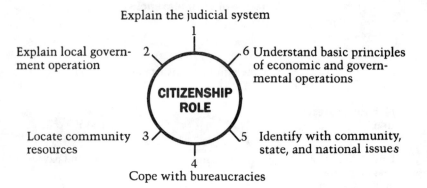

Explain the judicial system
1

Explain local govern- 2
ment operation

6 Understand basic principles
of economic and govern-
mental operations

**CITIZENSHIP
ROLE**

Locate community 3
resources

5 Identify with community,
state, and national issues

4
Cope with bureaucracies

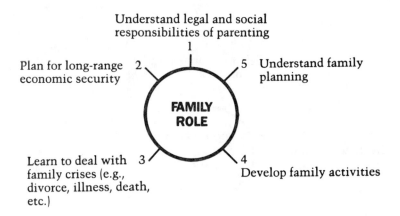

Understand legal and social
responsibilities of parenting
1

Plan for long-range 2
economic security

5 Understand family
planning

**FAMILY
ROLE**

Learn to deal with 3
family crises (e.g.,
divorce, illness, death,
etc.)

4
Develop family activities

68

Figure 9 continued

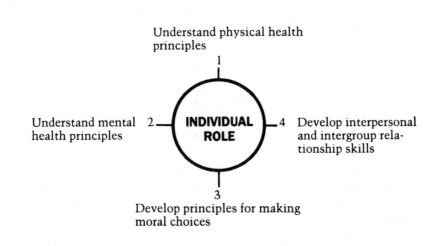

Some Characteristics of Careers Education

First and foremost, careers education is a learner-centered bridge between the time-honored subject-matter disciplines and the competencies required of an individual to cope with modern life. *It is an information-rich and experience-rich education based upon life-role proficiencies.*

Our daily lives do not fall neatly into math, social science, English, and science compartments. One great problem for the modern public schools is a lack of congruence between the traditional time-honored subject-matter disciplines and the competencies required to function in real life. In a careers-education program student competence is defined as demonstrated ability to apply knowledge, understanding, or skills assumed to contribute to success in life. Therefore, embedded deep within the philosophy of careers education is the idea that every student in elementary and secondary school must have the opportunity to develop the competencies required to function effectively in his

69

or her real-life roles. Thus, there is a profound shift in emphasis from what is to be taught to what is to be learned and to the outcomes of schooling. This is probably the most basic and powerful characteristic of a careers-education philosophy: it is real-life oriented and learner centered.

The second major characteristic of careers education is a clear policy demand. Educators seem strangely reluctant to talk about policy demands, but the schooling enterprise is chaotic unless a policy demand is made upon the school system and clear outcome signals are given. The school system is really not a system; it is a nonsystem. The only factors that hold this nonsystem together are many good teachers and good administrators working very hard. Every quality organization or system requires clear goals or targets. When the goals are fuzzy or out of focus, everything in the organization assumes the same image. As a result, the schools respond to real-life needs in all kinds of inconsistent ways. Some clear policy-demand signals are required.

The most positive effect of the careers-education movement may be its role in encouraging educators and the communities they serve to reexamine together what is to be taught and, more important, what is to be learned. This focus just may result in a greater degree of congruence between the expectations of students, the public, and the educators. Everyone will have a clearer picture of what the schools are to accomplish.

A renewed emphasis upon the expected outcomes of learning sets the stage for the introduction of careers education. A goal-based policy demand provides the framework for establishing, conceptualizing, and integrating the processes and procedures of careers education. Here is the kind of clear signal policymakers should consider writing into every policy handbook for schools:

> The education of the student results from a combined effort of home, church, community, schools, and the media. It shall be the responsibility of our schools to help students develop individual competencies to function in the career roles of learner, individual, wage earner, citizen, consumer, and family member.
>
> The schools have an important but shared responsibility and a secondary role in helping students develop social, emotional, cultural, and ethical/moral values. It is important that the schools

support and reinforce the home and other community institutions in these areas.

The first priority for the use of schooling resources shall be to help students develop the competencies to function as life-long learners.

This type of statement not only begins to make a policy demand upon the system, but also begins to define areas for which schools can be held accountable. Under the current system, schools are held accountable for results they haven't the remotest possibility of achieving. The schools must deal with goals that they are uniquely equipped, by training and by financing, to accomplish.

The third characteristic of careers education is a real-life orientation as expressed in life roles. The American public-school system operates within a web of "tensions." The major strand in this web of tensions is the relationship between individual and societal needs and the goals and activities of the schools. Much of what is done by the schools is done well, but the key question is, Should it be done at all? Are the schools addressing the highest priority needs?

Many of the major concerns in our society have no home in the modern school curriculum. Where is the home in the curriculum for environmental concerns? Is it in chemistry or biology or social science or business? Where is the home for consumer-education concerns? Is it in business or the social sciences or math? Where is the home for intergroup human relations concerns? What part of the school curriculum is responsible for helping people learn about dealing with their local government, voting on tax proposals, working with planning commissions? Where is the accountability in the modern school curriculum for helping a person develop the competencies to become a life-long learner, to analyze, to improve his or her memory? We often leave these vital concerns to chance and continue to insist on meeting the student at the point of some arbitrary subject-matter need rather than at the point of real-life needs.

The fourth characteristic of careers education is that less emphasis will be placed upon time. Students must be allowed to move and recycle through the instructional and evaluation process easily. Time must be used flexibly. Not all learners are nine-

71

week or eighteen-week learners. Rate of learning is the key difference among learners. Proponents of careers education are not as interested in how long it takes a student to master a given competency as they are in mastery itself.

A fifth characteristic of careers education is that clear expected outcome statements are placed "up front" as guides for both instructors and learners. There should be no surprises in the instructional or evaluation process. The instructor teaches to the goals, and the measurement and evaluation process occurs when learners demonstrate the ability to meet clearly defined outcome requirements. For example, when teaching swimming, the instructor teaches to the test by having the student swim from one end of the pool to the other. That is one clearly anticipated outcome, and there are no trick questions or surprises. The same can be said for computing interest rates or reading a newspaper or locating a book in a library.

Careers education does not turn its back on traditional subject matter or on time-honored instructional techniques; it only insists that the instructional program be based, at least in part, on real-life needs and that students demonstrate the applicability of what they have learned.

Perhaps now is also the time to rethink the purposes of the high-school graduation ceremony. *Wouldn't it be more meaningful for the high-school graduate to sit down with his or her parents, teachers, and perhaps a peer or two in a small group setting to demonstrate, as well as to discuss, his or her life-role competencies in a series of real-life tests?*

How Would Schooling Be Different With Careers Education?

Let us examine only one of the life roles, that of wage earner or producer, as an illustration. Let it be emphasized again that careers education is not synonymous with vocational education, although the latter is a significant aspect of careers education. American education has suffered from a misunderstanding of the place and value of vocational education. Unfortunately, the image in the minds of too many people is that vocational education is only specific job training. Instead, it is a way to help young people develop the competencies they need to be wage earners and producers. It is only one of several goals for schooling.

First, all of basic education must be infused with practical examples from the world of work and life roles. Even students in the primary grades must be able to see some relationship between what they are learning and the utility of that learning. Indeed, career awareness in the elementary schools should bring more life, more meaning, more experience, and more rigor to these early school experiences. Why not develop readers and library collections around world-of-work themes?

Second, career exploration in the middle grades can bring new purpose to those difficult adolescent years. Exploration does not mean that students will visit a little in the community or that they will talk a bit about jobs. Career exploration demands a rigorous multidisciplinary approach with industrial arts and homemaking teachers leading the way. The new pre-vocational program will explore all of the clusters and families of occupations, of which some fifteen to eighteen, with such titles as health occupations and mechanics occupations, are identified. Boys and girls in the middle years should be able to explore all of the clusters, not just some of them.

The challenge for the pre-vocational program is to bring more girls into the program and to provide a meaningful and rigorous middle-school curriculum. For example, in the world of construction, the building of a house can be a rich experience. Teachers must not only talk about the occupations involved in mixing mortar and cement, they must help students lay up a few bricks and experience the mixing of mortar. But that isn't all. The illustration of constructing a building provides tremendous opportunities for basic education. Who planned the building and how was the planning done. How was the money raised to pay for the building? What math is involved in building something? There are hundreds of real-life examples other than construction that could be utilized to bring life and experiences to the curriculum.

At the end of a three- or four-year period, students will have explored all the major clusters or families of occupation and have had actual lab experiences related to aspects of these occupations.

They also will have begun to understand the relationships between economics, mathematics, communications, and other disciplines.

Beginning with the eleventh grade, students would choose one of three curricular majors:

- a college-prep/baccalaureate-degree major
- a 2 + 2 tech-prep/associate-degree major
- a vocational cluster major

All three majors would focus on preparation for the next step for the student, whatever that step might be. All three majors would also include a common core of learning, including communication skills, social sciences, physical education. Mathematics and the physical/biological sciences would be tailored for each major. Allowances for individual differences in learning speed and style would be required in the common core. Wherever possible, common-core learning would be linked with real-life examples emanating from the careers-education emphasis.

The college-preparatory/baccalaureate-degree program would not vary much from the current grade eleven and twelve program except that a foreign language might be added where appropriate.

The tech-prep/associate-degree program would include a Principles of Technology course (applied physics) and some cooperative education and/or technical lab work along with the common core of learning. (The details of the program will be explained in Chapter VII.)

The vocational cluster program would include the common core of learning along with any of the career clusters for specific laboratory work, i.e., accounting, agriculture, clerical-secretarial, construction, electrical, food service, graphic arts, health services, marketing, mechanical, metals, transportation. The laboratory experiences would be built around the knowledge and skills common to the occupations that comprise the cluster or family of occupations.

The career-cluster program is not conceived as a means of developing a finished product or journeyman in any given occupation. Rather, it should provide opportunities for developing entry-level skills for certain jobs and some second-level skills for others. The result of the cluster effort should be that the student will enjoy greater flexibility in occupational choice patterns. Not only will students develop some entry-level skills, but they will also have an opportunity to appraise their own abilities in relation to several levels of occupations.

The Colorado Department of Education, under the leadership of Commissioner of Education Calvin Frazier, has added a significant dimension to the career-education program with the development of an "employability skills program." Since the fall of 1983, educators, employers, and community leaders in twelve Colorado communities have been engaged in the development of an employability/transition-skills effort. As a result of this effort, all high-school students will maintain a portfolio showing progress in attaining skills for transition to employment or post-secondary study. Upon graduation from high school, the student can present this portfolio to prospective employers and/or college personnel. (See form at conclusion of this chapter.)

As a postscript to this chapter, it is important to emphasize that careers education is also applicable to the collegiate curriculum. The Dallas County Community College District in Dallas, Texas, has been developing for several years a "Skills for Living"

Figure 10

Grades 11 and 12 Curriculum Structure

Two **Elective** **Courses**	
Five **Major** **Courses**	**Math** **Sciences** **Technical**
Five **Common Core** **Courses**	**Communication Skills** **Social Studies** **Physical Education**

common-learning program that forms the basic curricular goals of that large system of community colleges. After extensive review by faculty and administrative committees nine common learning goals have been developed and adopted:

1. *Living as a Learner*: Each DCCCD college will provide students opportunities to develop learning skills (reading, writing, speech communication, and computation) through assessment, advisement, and instruction.
2. *Living with Yourself*: Each DCCCD college will provide direction and opportunities for students to become more competent in developing themselves as individuals.
3. *Living with Others*: Each DCCCD college will provide opportunities for students to become more proficient in establishing and maintaining satisfying relationships with others.
4. *Living with Environments*: Each DCCCD college will provide opportunities for students to understand the relationship between individuals and their environments and make responsible decisions about the use of natural, human, technological, and spatial resources.
5. *Living as a Producer*: Each DCCCD college will provide opportunities for students to become more competent producers.
6. *Living as a Consumer*: Each DCCCD college will provide opportunities for students to become more competent as consumers.
7. *Living in the Community*: Each DCCCD college will provide opportunities for students to become more competent in using their skills and initiative to serve their local, national, and world communities and improve their quality of life.
8. *Living Creatively*: Each DCCCD college will provide opportunities for students to become proficient in the assessment, development, and application of their creative abilities.
9. *Living in the Future*: Each DCCCD college will provide opportunities for students to become more proficient in antici-

pating and accommodating change and to become more competent in examining possible alternatives for the future.

The Dallas County Community College District faculty have recognized that many common learning goals were already addressed throughout the curriculum. But it was difficult for faculty or students to determine with any degree of precision just how the goals were being met. It was felt that the "Skills for Living" goals could best be attained by identifying and developing common learning requirements. This requires the maintenance of several delicate balances throughout the college program. A balance must be maintained between:

- skill development and knowledge acquisition. The development of basic literacy skills, conceptual skills, and lifelong learning skills is fundamental to common learning in the community college, as is the mission of introducing knowledge likely to help students live with greater proficiency and humanity.
- training and education. The committee views as valuable both equipping students for work and expanding human understanding and vision.
- the structure of the curriculum which reflects the common learning commitments and the process of integrating this learning through curriculum review.
- the breadth and specificity of course and program content.
- choice and commonality. The college acknowledges student differences by offering learning and content choice balanced with a core of experiences common to all.
- student needs and external requirements of four-year institutions.

As the leaders of high schools and community colleges begin focusing upon careers education (whether it be called "skills for living," "life-role education," or "careers education"), it will be easier to bring continuity and coherence to the learning experience regardless of the educational level.

Figure 11

Identification of Essential Employability Skills

DIRECTIONS: Check those skills that are essential for students to acquire so that they will be well prepared to obtain employment and be successful on the job. In making judgments consider your own job experience. Add to part "M. Other" any skills which you consider essential which are not listed.

Name _____

Date _____

Please refer to the handout entitled "Identification of Employability Skills" for examples of each skill.

A. JOB SEEKING—CAREER DEVELOPMENT SKILLS
- [ ] 1. Knows sources of information
- [ ] 2. Knows own abilities, aptitudes, interests
- [ ] 3. Knows occupational characteristics
- [ ] 4. Identifies career/occupational goals
- [ ] 5. Develops a career plan
- [ ] 6. Identifies and researches potential employers
- [ ] 7. Knows employment position(s) desired
- [ ] 8. Accurately completes:
  - [ ] a. Inquiry letter
  - [ ] b. Resume
  - [ ] c. Follow-up letter
- [ ] 9. Accurately completes job application
- [ ] 10. Handles interview without errors
- [ ] 11. Seeks information about future education/training

B. MATH SKILLS
- [ ] 1. Understands importance of math in jobs
- [ ] 2. Performs basic calculations (+, −, ×, ÷)
- [ ] 3. Performs calculations in:
  - [ ] a. Fractions
  - [ ] b. Percentages
  - [ ] c. Proportions/Ratios
- [ ] 4. Makes reasonable estimates
- [ ] 5. Uses values from graphs, maps, tables
- [ ] 6. Uses English/metric measurement

- [ ] 7. Compares numerical values
- [ ] 8. Applies geometric principles
- [ ] 9. Uses formulas correctly
- [ ] 10. Constructs diagrams, tables, records
- [ ] 11. Uses elementary statistics
- [ ] 12. Uses instruments to solve problems:
  - [ ] a. Gauges, Meters, Scales
  - [ ] b. Calculators
  - [ ] c. Computers

C. COMPUTER SKILLS
- [ ] 1. Becomes aware of computer functions
- [ ] 2. Inputs and accesses data from computer
- [ ] 3. Has experience with computer programs
  - [ ] a. Business applications
  - [ ] b. Data management
  - [ ] c. Simple programming
  - [ ] d. Word processing
- [ ] 4. Understands issues associated with computer use

D. READING SKILLS
- [ ] 1. Understands the importance of reading in jobs
- [ ] 2. Develops vocabulary related to careers and occupations
- [ ] 3. Reads for details and special information
- [ ] 4. Interprets pictures, graphs, and symbols
- [ ] 5. Locates information in reference materials
- [ ] 6. Follows intent of written directions/instructions
- [ ] 7. Interprets ideas and concepts (comprehension)
- [ ] 8. Reads accurately at appropriate rate

78

Figure 11 continued

E. WRITING SKILLS
- [ ] 1. Understands the importance of writing in jobs
- [ ] 2. Develops handwriting legibility
- [ ] 3. Composes formal letters
- [ ] 4. Fills out forms
- [ ] 5. Records messages
- [ ] 6. Writes memorandums
- [ ] 7. Composes ads/telegrams
- [ ] 8. Writes instructions and directions
- [ ] 9. Writes reports
- [ ] 10. Develops summaries
- [ ] 11. Takes notes and/or outlines
- [ ] 12. Corrects written materials

F. COMMUNICATION SKILLS
- [ ] 1. Reports accurately/concisely
- [ ] 2. Follows intent of oral directions/instructions
- [ ] 3. Speaks distinctly
- [ ] 4. Formulates questions
- [ ] 5. Answers questions accurately
- [ ] 6. Explains activities and ideas clearly
- [ ] 7. Uses appropriate vocabulary/grammar
- [ ] 8. Gives clear instructions and directions
- [ ] 9. Stays on topic
- [ ] 10. Uses non-verbal signs appropriately
- [ ] 11. Develops oral presentations
- [ ] 12. Presents information effectively to groups

G. INTERPERSONAL SKILLS
- [ ] 1. Functions cooperatively with fellow students
- [ ] 2. Functions cooperatively in team efforts
- [ ] 3. Functions cooperatively with adults outside school
- [ ] 4. Exhibits openness and flexibility
- [ ] 5. Seeks clarification of instructions
- [ ] 6. Exercises patience and tolerance
- [ ] 7. Utilizes suggestions about improving skills
- [ ] 8. Uses initiative in getting work done
- [ ] 9. Expresses opinions with tact
- [ ] 10. Demonstrates ability to negotiate differences with others

H. BUSINESS ECONOMIC SKILLS
- [ ] 1. Understands business organization
- [ ] 2. Understands business competition
- [ ] 3. Knows about processes of marketing
- [ ] 4. Knows about processes of production
- [ ] 5. Understands business costs
- [ ] 6. Understands factors affecting profits

I. PERSONAL ECONOMIC SKILLS
- [ ] 1. Knows how to evaluate products and services
- [ ] 2. Knows how to access community resources/services
- [ ] 3. Can compute working hours/wages
- [ ] 4. Knows how to handle financial affairs
- [ ] 5. Can handle records of income and expenses
- [ ] 6. Knows how to make price-quality comparisons
- [ ] 7. Knows how to prepare state/federal tax forms
- [ ] 8. Can evaluate insurance programs
- [ ] 9. Knows how to determine credit costs
- [ ] 10. Understands legal rights in agreements
- [ ] 11. Maintains and utilizes various forms of transportation

J. MANUAL PERCEPTUAL SKILLS
- [ ] 1. Constructs/assembles materials
- [ ] 2. Uses specific hand tools and instruments
- [ ] 3. Develops visual presentations
- [ ] 4. Masters keyboard skills
- [ ] 5. Operates power equipment

K. WORK ACTIVITY SKILLS
- [ ] 1. Produces type/amount of work required
- [ ] 2. Maintains punctuality
- [ ] 3. Meets attendance requirements
- [ ] 4. Accepts assignments/responsibilities
- [ ] 5. Takes responsibility for own actions
- [ ] 6. Maintains consistent effort

Figure 11 continued

☐ 7. Works independently
☐ 8. Manages time effectively
☐ 9. Respects rights and property of others
☐ 10. Adheres to policies and regulations
☐ a. Health
☐ b. Honesty
☐ c. Safety
☐ 11. Presents a neat appearance
☐ 12. Keeps work area in good/safe condition
☐ 13. Exhibits interest in future career
☐ 14. Suggests or makes workplace improvements
☐ 15. Knows sources of continuing education
☐ 16. Knows about basic employee/student rights
☐ 17. Knows about basic employee/student responsibilities
☐ 18. Knows basic steps in getting a raise or promotion
☐ 19. Knows how to terminate employment

For the following section, evaluate in terms of projects that involve a full range of problem solving activities.

L. PROBLEM SOLVING/REASONING SKILLS
☐ 1. Recognizes problems that need solution

☐ 2. Identifies procedures
☐ 3. Obtains resources
☐ 4. Prepares or sets up materials/equipment
☐ 5. Collects information
☐ 6. Organizes information
☐ 7. Interprets information
☐ 8. Formulates alternative approaches
☐ 9. Selects efficient approaches
☐ 10. Reviews progress
☐ 11. Evaluates activities
☐ 12. Corrects errors
☐ 13. Makes conclusions
☐ 14. Summarizes and communicates results
☐ 15. Uses results to develop new ideas

M. OTHER
☐ 1. _____
☐ 2. _____
☐ 3. _____
☐ 4. _____
☐ 5. _____
☐ 6. _____
☐ 7. _____
☐ 8. _____
☐ 9. _____

Source: Colorado Department of Education

Community, Technical, and Junior Colleges and the Associate Degree: Opportunity With Excellence

The greatest American educational invention of the nineteenth century was the land-grant college. The greatest American educational invention of the twentieth century is the two-year community college.

John Gardner, *No Easy Victories*

Three important historical events have greatly influenced the course of higher education in America. The first was the establishment of the land-grant university in the 1860's combining theoretical and practical education. The agriculture slogan "making two blades of grass grow where one grew before" emerged from the work of these wonderful and serviceable universities and county extension-agent programs, as did the beginning of high technology.

The second event was the establishment of the G.I. Bill in the mid-1940's. America made an educational investment in the men and women who served in the armed forces, one which has been repaid many times over in increased earning power and consequent government revenue. It was during this post-war period that policymakers began to see education as an investment in human-resource development.

The third major event was the formation of the contemporary community college. Social historians have given scant attention to the development of the community, technical, and junior college. On July 13, 1946, President Harry Truman created the President's Commission on Higher Education, later known as the Truman Commission. In his letter appointing members to the Commission, he wrote: "Among the more specific questions with which I hope the Commission will concern itself are ways and means of expanding educational opportunities for all able young people; the adequacy of curricula, particularly in the fields of international affairs and social understanding; the desirability of establishing a series of intermediate technical institutes; the financial structure of higher education with particular reference to the requirements of the rapid expansion of physical facilities." (Vaughan 1983)

On December 11, 1947, approximately seventeen months after it was established, the Truman Commission issued its six-volume report entitled "Higher Education for American Democracy." The report expressed concern about the limited higher education opportunities for a large portion of the nation's citizens, and to correct this situation, called for the development of *community colleges* across the land. *The Truman Commission report became a blueprint for developing higher education in post-war America and in it the phrase "community college" first appeared.* (Incidentally, George B. Zook, the chairman of the Commission, was also the first chairman of the national assembly of junior college leaders which met in 1920 to form the American Association of Junior Colleges. In 1972 the name was changed to the American Association of Community and Junior Colleges.)

George Vaughan, President of Piedmont Virginia Community College, has written on the link between President Truman and the development of the community college. He states:

> The Commission's report and its acceptance by President Truman tied the community college closely to the thinking and prestige of the President's office. President Truman was familiar with the junior college and its national organization, the AAJC. In 1946 the President sent the following message to the Association's annual convention: "The extension of general education represented by the junior colleges in this country constitutes a real contribution to democracy in education. Social, economic, and political conditions prevailing throughout the world can be solved only in terms of a lengthened period of education made available to an increasing proportion of the population." . . . In retrospect, the Truman Commission's Report can indeed be viewed as the community college's manifesto.

When the report was prepared in 1947, two-year colleges' role in higher education undoubtedly would have been considered somewhat insignificant by today's figures. For example, in the 1947-48 academic year, there were a total of 651 junior colleges: 328 were public and 323 were private. Total enrollment was 500,536; of that number, 378,844 were in public colleges and 121,692 in private colleges.

Today there are 1,221 institutions; 1,066 public and 155 private. The 1983-84 year-long unduplicated headcount enrollment is estimated at 10,941,830 credit and non-credit students. Of that number, 10,707,876 were enrolled in public colleges and 233,954 in private colleges during the entire 1983-84 college year.

The American Association of Community and Junior Colleges offered a special tribute to President Truman at a national reception in honor of his 100th birthday in May of 1984, in cooperation with the Truman Centennial Committee. Here are some comments included in the special souvenir program prepared for that celebration:

- Senator Paul Simon *(Illinois)*
  The tremendous progress that community colleges have made in so short a time reflects upon the great good sense of President Harry S. Truman. In fact, today's concept of the community college is such a good fit that it is hard to imagine a higher education system without it.
- Former Senator and Senate Majority Leader Howard H. Baker, Jr. *(Tennessee)*
  I cannot think of a better tribute to President Truman than to recognize the bold steps he took to establish the community college network.
- Speaker of the House Thomas P. O'Neill, Jr. *(Massachusetts)*
  Fifty years ago this country was divided between two classes: the wealthy and the poor. Today, our country is dominated

Figure 12

Fifty Years of Growth in Two-Year College Credit Enrollments
1933–34 to 1983–84*

Number of Colleges				Enrollment		
Year	Public	Private	Total	Public	Private	Total
1933–34	223	309	532	77,111	33,138	110,249
1943–44	261	323	584	74,853	32,954	107,807
1953–54	327	267	594	533,008	69,856	602,864
1963–64	503	268	771	913,057	120,349	1,033,406
1973–74	910	231	1,141	2,729,685	136,377	2,866,062
1983–84	1,064	155	1,219	4,799,768	148,207	4,947,975

Does not include an estimated 1983–84 4.5 million non-credit enrollment and represents the enrollment for fall semester only.

Source: *American Association of Community and Junior Colleges*

by a great middle class. The biggest reason for this is education. Because of vital community colleges . . . millions of Americans have been given the opportunity not just to train themselves but also to become knowledgeable in the full range of human experience. Our country can be proud of this wonderful achievement. No other land in the world has made such a broad commitment to intellectual and economic opportunity.

- Former Congressman John Erlenborn *(Illinois)*
  I salute Harry S. Truman and the push his President's Commission on Higher Education gave the community college movement. Both have been good for America.
- Senator Mark O. Hatfield *(Oregon)*
  The Truman educational legacy began a new era in higher education. Indeed, the development of the two-year college system owes a great debt to his work to bring America out of war and into a productive society.
- Former Congressman the late Carl D. Perkins *(Kentucky)*
  In spite of the growth and strength of the community college system . . . the explosion of knowledge and the means of disseminating it make it essential that we strengthen this community institution to educate, re-educate, train, and retrain people several times during their lifetime in order to prepare them to participate effectively, not only in the workplace, but in society.
- Congressman Claude Pepper *(Florida)*
  As a member of the U.S. Senate when the Truman Commission issued its report, I was glad to be able to support the expansion of the community college system. This is an important part of the American dream.
- Senator Claiborne Pell *(Rhode Island)*
  The explosive growth of community and junior colleges and technical schools . . . [has] brought the dream of a post-high-school education within both the physical and financial reach of millions of Americans.
- Senator Orrin Hatch *(Utah)*
  One of the absolutely unique characteristics of most community colleges is their extraordinary ability to respond to

short-term training . . . Access to education governs the pace at which new knowledge is absorbed, [and] adjustments are made to new technologies.

- Senator Robert C. Byrd *(West Virginia)*
Harry S. Truman may have been the kind of man Thomas Jefferson had in mind when he praised the everyday American citizen as the keystone of our democracy . . . If any man looks for proof of Harry S. Truman's native wisdom and practical vision, he need search no further than the excellent community colleges whose seeds were sown during President Truman's years in the White House.

Community colleges have brought vocational and technical education into the halls of ivy-covered institutions. *These colleges have said there is dignity and worth in all honest labor.* They have also developed their own personalities and their own sense of mission. I may resemble or behave like someone else, but I have my own personality and my own definition of excellence. Such is the case with the community colleges. *They may look and act like other institutions of learning, but they have their own mission, built around the general theme of providing a host of Americans opportunity with excellence in pursuing a higher education.*

The phrase most often used to describe the American community college is "opportunity with excellence," while the word that best describes America is "opportunity." Think of the millions of immigrants who have come to this country because America remains the land of opportunity; opportunity is the very soul of the community college. These "people's colleges" provide opportunities for most of our citizens and endeavor to provide these opportunities in an excellent way.

When Lester Maddox was governor of Georgia, he was interviewed on network television. At the time, Georgia was having difficulties with its prison system. The reporter asked, "Governor Maddox, why are you having so much trouble in the prisons of Georgia?" Mr. Maddox leaned back in his chair and said with a smile, "The trouble with the Georgia prisons is that we need a better brand of prisoner." This appears to be the logic of some of the educational reformers on the scene today. If we could just get a "better brand of prisoner," if we just had tougher admissions standards, we could achieve excellence in our schools and colleges. Community, technical, and junior colleges have brashly challenged that definition of excellence. As "open door" institutions they have not placed the stress on entrance requirements but on exit requirements—upon the "value added" to the individual . . . and upon opportunity.

Belief is a powerful thing. Peter Marshall, the great chaplain of the U.S. Senate, said, "God help us to stand for something lest we fall for anything." It does make a difference what we believe, and it makes a powerful difference what a college or any public organization believes. The five most debilitating words in the English language are "it won't make any difference." *The community, technical, and junior colleges of this land are making a difference, not only in the lives of hundreds of thousands of citizens and individuals, but also in the life of our country.*

The Basic Elements of the "Opportunity With Excellence" Philosophy

Why did nearly nine million individuals take one or more college credit or non-credit classes during the 1984 fall term in a community, technical, or junior college? What are these colleges like? What are the characteristics of an excellent community college? What motivates the people that work and teach in these colleges?

There are five fundamental elements that generally characterize the excellent community college. *These five elements form the basis of the community college philosophy of education.* They are the articles of faith for those who live and work in these unique American institutions.

First among the five basic elements of this "opportunity with excellence" philosophy is the belief that community colleges must be *community-based.* They see themselves in partnership with the communities they serve. The fact that these colleges are often locally controlled gives them even deeper local roots.

In recent years these colleges have nearly become modern versions of the land-grant universities. They serve the public and private employers of a region. Nearly all of the 1,221 community, technical, and junior college campuses report some type of partnership arrangement with employers and others in the community. Community, technical, and junior colleges have a long history of working effectively with local community organizations as well as with local employer and employee organizations. Nearly all the occupational-education programs are supported and advised by advisory committees composed of community professionals working in specific occupational areas related to a specific curriculum. In fact, community colleges often utilize the expertise of local citizens by bringing them into the faculty as part-time instructors. (See Figure 13.) Thus, the town-and-gown barrier has been effectively removed.

The community-college school day is a long one, and the average age of its students is twenty-nine. If you visit a community college at eight in the evening you will see a much older adult population being served than at eight in the morning. Life-long learning in action can be observed in these community-based institutions.

The roots of the community college grow deep in the high schools that feed students into the college. Too often, in times past, some community colleges have paid insufficient attention to developing partnership arrangements with these high schools. That concern forms much of the focus of this book. *The "opportunity with excellence" theme is greatly diminished unless community, technical, and junior colleges coordinate their programs with the feeder high schools.*

A key word in the community college-community-based philosophy is *access*. There is strong evidence that geographical access to classes makes a considerable difference in the rate of

Figure 13

Comparison of 1982 and 1983 Professional Personnel in Community, Technical, and Junior Colleges

	Faculty Full-time	Faculty Part-time	Total	Adm. Staff	Other Prof. Staff
1982	109,812	137,060	246,872	18,634	16,185
1983	109,436	142,170	251,606	18,228	17,147
% change	− .34	+ 3.73	+ 1.92	− 2.18	+ 5.94

89

college attendance. Where the college campus is far away or where the classes are not held at convenient times, the rate of attendance is much lower than when the reverse is true. A community-based characteristic of the community college is that it does not insist that all students come to a central campus. Education and training are brought to the student in local businesses, churches, high schools, union halls, and shopping centers, at all times of the day or evening. *The community college has broken the barriers of time and space in the delivery of educational services.*

The second element of the "opportunity with excellence" philosophy is *cost effectiveness*. Community colleges endeavor to stay within the financial reach of their students. They endeavor to maintain low costs and low tuition.

The average 1984-85 student tuition in the community colleges across the country was $600. Although the amount may vary from state to state, it is an article of faith that the commu-

Figure 14

Community, Technical and Junior College Locations

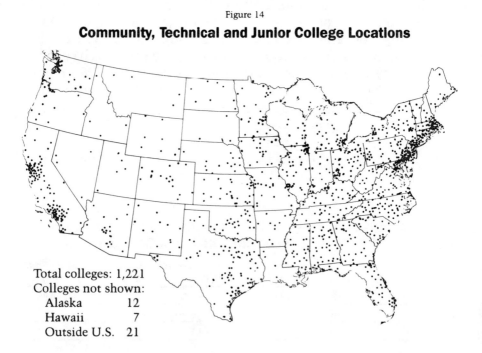

Total colleges: 1,221
Colleges not shown:
    Alaska   12
    Hawaii   7
    Outside U.S. 21

90

nity college tuition remain low. The low tuition combined with state and federal financial-aid programs ensures that these colleges are financially accessible to most of the citizens they serve. Even in financially difficult times community college leaders will go to any lengths to avoid raising student-tuition rates.

A second aspect of the cost-effectiveness tenet is low operating costs. Not only do community college leaders work hard at maintaining low student costs, they also work hard at maintaining low taxpayer costs. Figure 15 gives the comparative operating costs and tuition charges for various institutions of higher education. Community, technical, and junior colleges are the low-cost institutions in higher education.

Continuing efforts are made to trim and modernize operating costs in community colleges. Each year the National Association of College and University Business Officers in cooperation with the U.S. Steel Corporation sponsors a national competition among colleges and universities to encourage innovative cost-containment ideas. Lane Community College in Eugene, Oregon, has won the national competition two out of three years. Community, technical, and junior colleges always do well in this competition. This observation does not mean that other colleges and universities are not concerned about cost-containment practices; they all are! But because the community college is a teaching institution without a research mission, and because there is intense local interest in the work of these colleges, the operating costs tend to be lower.

Figure 15

College and University Full-Time Equivalent per Student Operating Expenditures: National Average 1980–81

Control	University	Four-Year College	Two-Year College
Public	$ 9,725	$7,246	$3,061
Private	16,977	7,764	3,514

College and University Tuition and Fees 1980–81			
Public	$1,270	$1,020	$ 510
Private	6,140	4,750	3,300

Source. U.S. Department of Education, National Center for Education Statistics

The third element of the "opportunity with excellence" philosophy in a community college is a *caring environment*. We haven't talked enough in higher education about that. John Naisbitt writes about the "high tech/high touch" society in which we live:

> Much has been written about the human potential movement, but to my knowledge no one has connected it with technological change. In reality, each feeds the other, high tech/high touch.
>
> Now, at the dawn of the twenty-first century, high tech/high touch has truly come of age. Technology and our human potential are the two great challenges and adventures facing humankind today. The great lesson we must learn from the principle of high tech/high touch is a modern version of the ancient Greek ideal—balance. We must learn to balance the material wonders of technology with the spiritual demands of our human nature. (Naisbitt, *Megatrends*, 1984)

On campuses, in classrooms, in counseling centers, at admissions windows, and in administrative offices of the community college the student usually finds a caring environment.

The typical image of a college student is a nineteen-year-old recent high-school graduate attending school full time. But the community college student is often quite different. Community colleges serve recent high-school graduates and serve them well, but they also serve part-time students and adults. There is a tremendously diverse population in the community college, and providing a caring environment for that diversity may be its greatest strength.

The need for a caring environment is everywhere: in schools, stores, unions, and businesses. The more technology that is thrown at us, the greater our need for caring, for human touch, for kindness, for respect, for self-esteem. This need should not be left up to the counselors to fulfill. Each individual who enrolls in a class or comes to the campus must feel that the college really cares about him or her as an individual. Community colleges work hard at meeting this responsibility, and partially measure their effectiveness against the degree to which they have established and maintained a caring environment.

Special commendation must be given the community college student-personnel professionals. As a relatively new seventy-five-year-old profession, college counseling has struggled to establish its legitimacy in higher education. In recent years, counselors have struggled even more with budget cutbacks and staff reductions. Although some new student personnel service models may be in order, it is these professionals who have established and maintained the "caring environment" emphasis in the community, technical, and junior colleges.

Necessity is certainly the mother of invention, and survival has been a motivator among college student-personnel workers. A variety of strategies have been developed to help students succeed in completing their community college courses. Testing and early-placement efforts are blossoming. Orientation programs, particularly for high-risk students, are being developed. Early intervention and tutorial services are becoming common. Integrated student-support services covering orientation, early intervention, tutorial services, developmental education, learning resources, and other retention services show much promise. Arthur Cohen speaks to this point:

> Retention is a multifaceted dimension. It begins with student recruitment and ends with follow-up activities that provide assistance in making choices of program, on-campus work opportunities, transfer institution, and career employment. Recruitment can be enhanced if honors programs are built; the community colleges need the best students as well as the worst. Pre-school orientation has also proved useful along with the type of continuing support that says to the student, "We care." Students no longer have the right to fail. The coming decade will see attrition rates decline and transfer and career success increase. (Cohen 1984-85)

Community colleges do not pride themselves on how many students fail, but rather they rejoice at how many succeed. *In the absence of a caring environment that places great emphasis upon individual student success, excellence can be smothered easily by the weeds of an impersonal "business as usual."*

The fourth crucial element of the "opportunity with excellence" philosophy is a *competent faculty.* These are the individuals who are at the center of the caring environment.

93

Folk wisdom has it that teachers are a generally dissatisfied lot and that many community college faculty members, who would prefer to be teaching in universities, are the most dissatisfied of all. George Riday, Professor of Psychology at Citrus Community College in California, and two of his colleagues decided to find the truth. They compared the degree of job satisfaction/dissatisfaction among secondary-school faculty, community college faculty, and four-year college and university faculty. What they found was that teaching is a satisfying and fulfilling profession regardless of teaching level and that community college faculty ranked the highest on the faculty-satisfaction scale.

A close view of the specific scale areas and items on the survey instrument yields insights into some of the sources of satisfaction for community-college teachers. They highly value the feeling of achievement and accomplishment in their personal progress and in the performance of their students. They prize their association with their students and colleagues, they enjoy being a part of the campus environment, and they feel recognized and rewarded. The work itself is highly satisfying, and the conditions under which

Figure 16

Comparison of Mean Satisfaction Scores on the WS/DS Among Secondary School (SS), Community College (CC), and Four-Year College (4Y) Teachers

Composite Scales	Mean Satisfaction		
	SS	CC	4Y
Achievement	4.3	4.9	4.5
Growth	3.5	4.0	4.1
Interpersonal relations	4.7	5.2	4.8
Policy/administration	3.4	3.9	3.9
Recognition	4.1	4.4	4.4
Responsibility	4.3	4.8	4.6
Salary	2.7	3.7	2.8
Supervision	3.7	4.2	4.2
Work itself	4.8	5.5	5.2
Working conditions	4.1	4.6	4.1

Source: Riday et al.

they work are favorable . . . The community college offers a setting where the faculty may justifiably feel that they have a teaching career worthy in its own right, not a stepping stone to a higher level of education. Clearly the community college need not perceive itself "junior" to the four-year collegiate institution with respect to job satisfaction of faculty. (Riday et al. 1984-85)

The findings of this study confirm my own experiences. *Some of the best teaching I have seen and some of the most dedicated and caring faculty members I have met are in the community colleges.*

This brings us to the fifth element of the "opportunity with excellence" philosophy. These colleges believe in a *comprehensive community college program* with the liberal-arts and technical-education programs working in a thoroughly integrated manner. What is "vocational" in today's job market? There is nothing more "vocational" than Spanish classes for a law enforcement officer in some of our communities. In that sense, foreign language courses are "vocational." What is more "vocational" than speaking and analytical skills for a salesperson?

The comprehensive community college program is under attack in some state capitals across the country. State-level leaders are asking if they can afford a comprehensive community college program. The answer is simple: we cannot afford *not* to have such a program. The costs are too great. If community colleges are to meet students at the point of student need, if they are to place the student at the center of their concerns, a comprehensive program is absolutely mandatory. The good jobs of the future will demand workers from comprehensive programs. In today's technological society colleges simply cannot have first-rate technical-education programs unless they are integrated with liberal-arts programs. A first-rate technical-education program requires an extensive math, science, and literacy base, an understanding of our economic system, and some exposure to cultures other than our own. Community, technical, and junior colleges have brought vocational education into the ivy-covered walls of the collegiate world.

The real competition for jobs in the future will be between the well-educated and the not-so-well-educated. Less-educated workers are at a real disadvantage if the unemployment rate is any indication. In 1982 the unemployment rate among the twenty- to twenty-four-year-olds with less than four years of high school was thirty-two percent. The rate among high-school graduates was fifteen percent, while unemployment rates for those with one to three years of college and four or more years of college were nine percent and six percent respectively: "The connection between higher unemployment rates and low levels of education shows the importance of education in a job market that increas- ingly requires more training." (*Occupational Outlook Hand- book* 1984)

The number of jobs that require some college education is projected to increase by forty-five percent over the 1982-95 period compared to the twenty-five-percent growth projected for all jobs over this same period. Employment executives of large corpora- tions report a shortage of technicians and skilled workers despite high unemployment. Deutsch, Shea and Evans, Inc., Human Resources Consultants, recently surveyed ninety-five firms and found shortages of electronic and electrical technicians, numer- ically controlled machine maintenance and repair workers, heat- ing, ventilating, and air-conditioning technicians, and such pro- duction workers as tool and die makers and machinists. *Com- munity colleges are taking on the task of helping to supply America with a skilled and knowledgeable work force.*

To meet the needs of its student body, the community college has developed a variety of programs. The college-transfer program is designed to equip students with the knowledge and credits to transfer to a four-year college or university and to pursue a bac- calaureate degree. The junior college (and now the community college) has always offered an excellent university-parallel pro- gram with first-rate "teaching" professors. Most colleges and states have now developed college-credit transfer-articulation agreements that allow students to transfer credits without slip- page. How well do community college students do in the uni- versity?

Piedmont Virginia Community College conducted a perfor- mance study of its graduates who transferred to the University of Virginia between 1978 and 1983, with the following results:

PVCC graduates who transferred and spent their junior and senior years at the University of Virginia slightly out-performed their classmates who entered the University as freshmen. PVCC transfers earned a 3.15 grade-point average at UVA; students who entered UVA as freshmen had a 3.09 average. The average age of PVCC students transferring to UVA was almost twenty-eight. Some had been out of school for fifteen years; at least two had earned GED's (high-school equivalency diplomas) prior to entering PVCC. Twenty percent of the PVCC transfers had previously been denied admission to UVA as freshmen. Many of these students started at levels well below those of UVA's regular-admission students, but they had achieved parity by the end of the junior year.

Santa Fe Community College of Gainesville, Florida, offers academic scholarships to the top ten percent of each graduating class of the eight feeder high schools. In 1984, forty-five percent, including four of the eight valedictorians, accepted these scholarships and chose Santa Fe Community College. Many of these students, whose combined SAT scores ran as high as 1270, turned down other scholarships. It should also be noted that Santa Fe Community College is in the same town as the University of Florida, which also aggressively recruits academically talented students.

These are not isolated stories. *Increasingly, strong academic students are choosing the community college for their first college experience.* As community colleges install honors programs and become more aggressive in seeking out these students, their numbers will continue to grow in the community college ranks.

The community college transfer program also provides a second chance for many students: those who, for all kinds of reasons, did not succeed their first time around in the traditional four-year college or university. As the community college accepts them with open arms and provides additional learning support services, these students find they can now succeed in baccalaureate-degree programs.

Finally, the college-transfer curriculum provides that common core of learning so essential to any college student. The humanities, the liberal arts, the fine arts, are as important to the elec-

97

tronic technician as they are to the engineer. *Caring, compassion, and understanding, the central focus of a liberal education, can help all of us who live and struggle together on this single globe called Earth.*

The developmental-education program helps individuals develop the proficiencies to be life-long learners. It also helps individuals remove the educational barriers that impede progress toward their goals. That barrier may be reading speed, or writing skills, or computational deficiencies, or memory training, or problem-solving skills, or analytical skills. The emphasis in developmental education is on diagnosis, prescription, and program placement. This program is vital to the success of the open-door colleges. Some colleges refer to the program as college preparatory, as it helps individuals develop the knowledge and skills to negotiate college-level work.

The adult and continuing-education program is basically non-credit and particularly designed for individuals who desire to learn for the sake of learning, to upgrade themselves, to acquire a new skill, or in some cases for job retraining. Much of the continuing-education program is built around the notion of occupational extension. In the past there have been few educational extension opportunities for those occupations which require less than a bachelor's degree for job entry. In this modern information age there are almost endless adult and continuing education needs in the ever-changing field of occupational upgrading and retraining.

The community-service program is another important aspect of the continuing-education program. As an example, in our multicultural and diverse society, community colleges have said we dare not leave the fine arts and lecture series to those institutions serving only the university community.

Finally, one of the continuing intractable problems confronting our society is the need to help the victims of socio-economic deprivation to develop the basic educational skills so desperately required to move on to a baccalaureate degree and/or to succeed in an occupation. Community, technical, and junior colleges have their collective sleeves rolled up and are heavily involved in the task of helping the socio-economically disadvantaged remove their educational barriers and move into the economic mainstream of American life.

That is the template of excellence to lay over the work of the community colleges. *They are community based, they are cost effective, they offer a nurturing and caring environment, they pride themselves on having a competent faculty, and they offer a comprehensive program to meet an assortment of educational needs.*

Community, technical, and junior colleges are a vast and growing force in America. They enroll a stunning fifty-five percent of all the freshmen in institutions of higher learning across the country today. Approximately eight percent of all adult Americans will take one or more classes in an American community, technical, or junior college this year. These institutions are acting out and modeling our national commitments.

In a nation with a moral commitment to access and opportunity, community colleges are the accessible institutions. In a nation with a tremendous need for skilled workers, community colleges are fulfilling that need. They are helping a host of citizens discover that marketable skills give them liberating competence and the confidence that they can do something well— that they can cope with real life. In a nation leading in information-age development, community colleges are the institutions that are helping trigger economic revitalization by matching skills to the needs of the employers. In a nation that emphasizes accountability, community colleges are a cost-effective part of higher education. In a nation deeply concerned about the quality of life, community colleges are leading the way by providing quality-of-life experiences for all levels of working men and women across this great nation.

Community, technical, and junior colleges are making history. George Wythe, a lawyer at William and Mary College, said to his student and friend, Thomas Jefferson, "Preach, my dear friend, preach a crusade against ignorance." And that is the slogan of the community colleges. *They are crusading against ignorance— against wasted lives. They are providing opportunity with excellence across America.*

99

What Is the Associate Degree?

Although the associate degree has been in existence for eighty-five years, it has not become well known until the past twenty. The arrival of the information age and the proliferation of technician-level education programs have spurred interest in this two-year degree. They have also led to the establishment of a variety of associate degrees: associate in arts, associate in science, associate in applied science, associate in computer science, associate in business, and the like. In fact, suggestions are being made today from those representing some four-year colleges and universities to require the associate degree of all those pursuing the baccalaureate degree.

Leslie Koltai, Chancellor of the Los Angeles Community College District, reports as follows:

> The American community college is becoming one of the most successful educational institutions in the world. Many developing countries have already adopted models of community and/or technical colleges and have created hundreds of institutions to usher in a new age of civilization.
>
> In the United States the community college is a growing educational enterprise . . . During the last decade the number of associate degrees awarded increased by approximately sixty percent, compared with an increase of eleven percent for the baccalaureate degree. In fact, associate degrees, which accounted for more than eighteen percent of all degrees in 1970, grew to twenty-three percent at the end of the decade. (Koltai 1984)

The public also have given community, technical, and junior colleges and the associate degree a vote of confidence. The American Association of Community and Junior Colleges, along with the College Board and the Council for Advancement and Support of Education, commissioned Group Attitudes Corporation of New York in 1984 to conduct a random-sample public-opinion telephone survey of 1,006 persons age eighteen or older. One principal finding of the survey was that Americans show great confidence in community, technical, and junior colleges and believe that they offer quality education at a reasonable cost. Four out of five individuals polled (80.9 percent) felt that an associate degree from a community college is useful in helping a person

100

transfer to a four-year college or university. Three out of four (75.9 percent) felt that such a degree is useful in helping a person get a job that requires some expertise or training.

The Associate Degree Policy Statement

In order to send clear signals on a national level, the American Association of Community and Junior Colleges Board of Directors adopted a policy statement on the associate degree in July 1984. Under the leadership of Leslie Koltai, Chancellor of the Los Angeles Community College District, Harold McAninch, President of the College of DuPage in Illinois, and Ernest Boyer, President of the Carnegie Foundation for the Advancement of Teaching, this statement was developed after eighteen months of debate and discussion.

AMERICAN ASSOCIATION OF COMMUNITY AND JUNIOR COLLEGES
Policy Statement on the Associate Degree

The Associate Degree

The associate-degree program is reaffirmed as central to the mission of the community, technical, and junior college. The associate degree reflects the larger goals of educational attainment the institution holds for its students. It is a means through which the institution develops and maintains integrity in its educational programs. When appropriately defined, the associate degree becomes an integrating force for the institution, serves as an important student guide, and requires commitment on the part of the student for program completion.

Emphasis on the associate-degree program indicates to faculty, administrators, students, and society that the community, technical, and junior colleges have a vision of what it means to be an educated person and affirm the colleges' commitment to program continuity, coherence, and completion. The associate degree must indicate that the holder has developed proficiencies sufficient to prepare for upper-division collegiate work, or to enter directly into a specific occupation with confidence. The degree should be

101

awarded only for completion of a coherent program of study designed for a specific purpose.

The Responsibility for Quality

The institution offering an associate degree assumes a responsibility to students and the public to establish and maintain excellence in all educational programs. In offering such a degree program, the individual institution recognizes the obligation to certify that the student receiving the degree has indeed attained associate-degree levels of achievement. When an institution awards the associate degree it is providing the individual with the currency to negotiate the next step, whether that step be into full-time employment or into a baccalaureate-degree program. The associate degree should be recognized by employers and baccalaureate-degree-granting institutions as the best indication that a student has attained the knowledge and skills necessary to enter a field of work or an upper-division college program.

Quality community, technical, and junior colleges demand substantial investments, and the investments return great dividends to individuals and to our nation. Because of the investment required to build and maintain a quality program, the institution has a professional obligation to develop programs where resources are sufficient to ensure quality. In addition, the institution, in partnership with the communities it serves, must provide straightforward information to appropriate decision makers about the resources required to maintain a quality program.

Organization of the Curriculum

Working under the direction of the appropriate administrative leaders, the teaching faculty and academic staff have the responsibility to design, monitor, and evaluate the specific associate-degree programs offered by the institution. This process should involve consultation with others, both inside and outside the institution. The associate-degree program links learning that has gone before with learning that will come after. Therefore, those concerned with framing the associate-degree requirements must not approach the task in isolation. Full attention must be given to continuity in learning, as well as to the proficiencies required for an individual to achieve career satisfaction. Community college leaders are encouraged to maintain a continuing dialogue with high-school administrators and faculty, as well as with college and university decision makers, with regard to program scope and sequence. The students should experience little or no loss of continuity, or loss of credits, when moving from one level of education to another.

The resulting associate-degree program should consist of a coherent and tightly knit sequence of courses capped by an evaluation process, either at the course level, comprehensively, or both. All degree programs must include the opportunity for the students to demonstrate proficiency in the use of language and computation, for whatever their career goals, students will be called upon to exercise competence in these areas.

In addition, all associate-degree programs should reflect those characteristics that help define what constitutes an educated person. Such characteristics include a level of general education that enables the individual to understand and appreciate his/her culture and environment; the development of a system of personal values based on accepted ethics that lead to civic and social responsibility; the attainment of skills in analysis, communication, quantification, and synthesis necessary for further growth as a lifespan learner and a productive member of society. It is understood that not all these elements are attained fully through organized courses, but that the intellectual and social climate of the institution and the variety of other educational activities engaged in by students may play an important part. It is incumbent upon the institution to develop appropriate procedures to assess required learning gained outside the formal course structure.

The Associate in Arts and Associate in Science Degree

These degrees prepare the student primarily for transfer to an upper-division baccalaureate-degree program. Programs leading to these degrees are similar in nature. The general trend has been to offer the associate in science degree to students who wish to major in engineering, agriculture, or the sciences with heavy undergraduate requirements in mathematics and science. The associate in arts degree is directed to those majoring in the social sciences, humanities, arts, and similar subjects. However, it should be noted that the distinction between the two degrees and the eventual baccalaureate major has become somewhat blurred in recent years. Students awarded associate in arts or associate in science degrees should be accepted as junior-level transfers in baccalaureate-degree-granting institutions.

Associate in Applied Science Degree

The second type of degree program is destined to lead the individual directly to employment in a specific career. While the titles given these degrees vary considerably among community, technical, and junior colleges, the most common title is associate in applied science. Other titles used are associate in business, associate in data processing, or other specific occupations, and associate in applied arts and sciences. It should be noted that the number of degrees awarded in these occupational areas has been increasing in the last two decades. In some instances, particularly in the health-related fields, the degree is a prerequisite for taking a licensing examination. Some institutions belong to voluntary specialized accrediting agencies that set qualitative and quantitative degree standards for their programs. Although the objective of the associate in applied science degree is to enhance employment opportunities, some baccalaureate-degree-granting institutions have developed upper-division programs to recognize this degree for transfer of credits. This trend is applauded and encouraged.

Associate Degree Titles

In recent years there has been a proliferation of titles of associate degrees. This has been true especially in occupational areas where some institutions offer many different degrees in specific technologies. In an attempt to reduce the number of these degrees and to avoid confusion as to the level of academic achievement attained, it is highly recommended that:

(a) The titles "associate in arts" and "associate in science" degrees be used without further designation.

(b) The associate in applied science degree may have additional designations to denote special fields of study such as nursing, computer technology, or law enforcement.

(c) For all associate degrees the transcript of a student should reveal the exact nature of the program completed and whether courses are recommended for transfer to baccalaureate-degree programs.

(d) The names or designations used for associate degree be limited to the above three titles.

Guidelines for the Evaluation of Programs

Many factors may enter into the evaluation of associate-degree programs. The most basic and important elements relate to the objectives the institution itself has set for the degree program. Does the program, for example, provide the foundation in general education the institution has set as a goal? Does the program provide students with the competencies required to compete successfully in a career role? The evaluation of degree programs should create a continuing dialogue with the institution concerning associate-degree quality, and the relative success of the college's graduates must not be overlooked as a necessary evaluation tool.

Ideally, the evaluation of associate-degree programs in community, technical, and junior colleges should be accomplished by the institutions themselves and not by state or federal agencies. Regional accrediting associations serve as self-regulatory bodies to help institutions monitor and evaluate the quality of their associate-degree programs. In order that accountability for such evaluations may be clearly understood, institutions should designate institution-wide oversight bodies to evaluate the continuing balance and quality of associate-degree programs.

Looking Ahead

This policy statement is limited to the associate degree, thus leaving unexamined a host of other important elements of the community, technical, and junior college mission. These institutions are attended by many individuals for valid reasons other than obtaining a degree. Continuing education and noncredit courses are also reaffirmed as important to the mission of community, technical, and junior colleges. Nothing in this policy statement should be interpreted as discouraging colleges from admitting students who do not have degree objectives to all courses for which they are qualified and from which they will benefit.

While this policy statement is limited to a definition of the associate degree, it is recognized that further work should be pursued to define other community college outcome measures. Such study is important to the future of community, technical, and junior colleges, particularly as they attempt to influence funding agencies and legislators, and to meet a great diversity of individual human need.

Adopted by the American Association of Community and Junior Colleges Board of Directors, July 7, 1984

Chapter VI

The High-School/ Community College Connection

Vocational/technical training has been community colleges' outstanding success, but you have not thought out your linkage with high schools.

Governor Bruce Babbitt, Arizona

A bold headline in the July 27, 1984, edition of *USA Today* proclaimed: "Freshmen: Fuzzy Ideas About College." The article indicated that high-school students entering college have little or no idea of what to expect once they are enrolled and that most colleges are not doing a very good job of helping high-school students develop a realistic idea of what it takes to succeed in a college program. A survey was conducted by James Kelly of Pennsylvania State University involving some 18,000 incoming college freshmen in 1982 and 1983. Nearly all of the entering freshmen, ninety-eight percent, said they expected to earn a B average or better in college. At the same time, sixty-one percent of these students estimated they would study fewer than twenty hours per week. More than eighty percent said they knew little or nothing about their choice of major. Nearly half these entering freshmen listed "no one" as their main influence in choosing their major. (Kelly 1983)

It is obvious that few high-school students know how much work or what levels of proficiency will be required to complete a college program. They often know about entry standards, but few know about college exit requirements. The Kelly study was aimed primarily at students in four-year colleges, with only ten percent of the sample including students in two-year colleges. The matter then becomes truly serious for an open-door, open-admissions college. *It is the rare high-school student who has more than a vague notion of what an adequate high-school preparatory program is all about and how he or she can best prepare to succeed in a community, technical, or junior college program.*

Indeed, some high-school students seem to interpret the phrase "open-door college" as an invitation to expend a minimum amount of effort in high school; one need not prepare for the next step at all! The feeling seems to be, "I can always get into a community college." Few seem to know or worry about what it takes to exit a community college program. *So much attention has been given to college admissions that college exit requirements have been overlooked and shortchanged.*

Have community, technical, and junior colleges failed to give high-school students and their parents clear signals as to what constitutes an adequate high-school program of preparation for a career, as well as for university-parallel programs? Do open-door colleges have a responsibility to state clearly to high-school students the exit requirements for each and every community college program including the requirements to earn an associate degree? The answer is an unequivocal yes!

Community, technical, and junior colleges should be proud of their open-door label. They have opened the doors of opportunity for millions of Americans. Higher education will never be the same because of these open doors, and they must remain open. But the open-admissions policy has given some high-school students an unintended negative signal. For these students the open door becomes a revolving door—easy in and quickly out. The open door has never meant that high-school students can prepare or not, as they please, and still succeed in a community college program.

High-school students and their parents as well as high-school faculty and counselors deserve to know about community college exit standards, associate-degree requirements, study requirements; in short, about the rigors of completing any community college program. The reluctance of some community, technical, and junior college leaders to be directive in their communications with their high-school colleagues may have been honorable in intent. They have not wanted to be overbearing or appear to be telling another segment of education how to run its business. But they should know that most high-school administrators have no such fear. Indeed, high-school leaders are looking to higher education at all levels for clarity in communications about the preparation requirements that will help students succeed in their next steps. The student must be placed at the center of concern.

Too often in education we meet the student at the point of administrator need or faculty need or trustee need, rather than at the point of student need. In fact, the greatest single weakness of the host of reform reports has been lack of attention given the learner. What are the incentives that will motivate the learner toward excellence in learning? Do college requirements really have much influence on the high-school program and high-school student choices? There can be no question that colleges are a vital link in the critical chain of influence upon the high-school program. Sol Levine, Principal of Beverly Hills High School in California, comments on this point:

> My own experience on two ends of the continent—New York and California—leads me to believe that college admission standards can be a vital ingredient in shaping the secondary program. Properly developed and applied, they are intrusive. They force change. Further, I believe that it is an error to assume that the prestigious universities have a major impact on the four-year high-school program . . . the state and local colleges most clearly affect the largest percentage of high-school graduates. It is with an eye on the admission standards of these schools that most students develop their four-year high-school program . . . It was the requirements of the City University of New York which had a significant impact on the courses I took in high school. I, and most of my graduating class, saw the City University as the avenue for our higher education. I have little doubt that the adoption of the open admissions policy in later years had its own deep impact on the school program. (Levine 1984)

Community colleges, along with other postsecondary institutions, can play a significant role in helping to build public confidence in our schools. But more important, they can help many more high-school students raise their academic and vocational sights toward excellence. However, this will require cooperation. *It is time to build a more effective partnership between secondary schools and community, technical, and junior colleges.*

Raising high-school graduation requirements alone is not enough. Raising overall college-admission requirements misses the mark for the "open door" colleges, and raising individual college-program requirements is only a partial solution. Reform efforts absolutely require secondary and postsecondary schools and colleges to work together to improve the structure and the substance of learning for the ordinary student as well as for the baccalaureate-degree-track student. This will require some direct and open communication about college-program exit standards. *The concentration of cooperative effort between high schools and community colleges must emphasize what it takes to successfully complete a program rather than just emphasize entry requirements.*

It is important to point out that many people misinterpret the open-door college to mean that little attention is given to admission standards. Many community college programs such as nursing, some of the technologies, and the university-parallel program require that students meet certain criteria for admission. The "open door" means primarily opportunity. The community college endeavors to provide a variety of support services and learning opportunities to meet a great diversity of individual talents, hopes, and aspirations.

The challenge for the open-door and open-admissions college is to address the concept of excellence on its own terms. *The community college has a unique personality and mission.* It is a distinctive and relatively new partner in higher education. Excellence for the community, technical, and junior college must be achieved within the context of its own mission and purpose.

New models of excellence and new configurations will occur only when the needs of the students are placed above special-interest claims. In some ways the community college operates like the university, while in others, it has a mission similar to that of the comprehensive high school. However, mirroring pale imitations of the university or the high school will not meet the challenges of a highly diverse adult student body. In many ways the community college is developing into a contemporary version of the land-grant college, connecting the practical with the theoretical and connecting the community with the academic talent and resources of the college.

One of the vital elements of the community to be served by the community college is the high school. Community colleges must never forget that their roots are in the local high schools.

Community college and high-school personnel of the same region must establish deep and lasting linkages that will produce higher academic performance and stronger career/vocational programs.

In a 1983 speech at the Association of Community College Trustees meeting in Phoenix, Arizona, Governor Bruce Babbitt put it this way: "Vocational/technical education and training has been the outstanding success of the community colleges, but you have not thought out your linkages with the high schools."

Clifford Adelman, senior associate with the National Institute of Education and senior staff member serving the National Commission on Excellence, has concluded, after viewing much data, that local colleges, like community colleges, have a significant influence on the curriculum choices of high-school students:

> The more proximate the postsecondary institution is to the secondary school, the more likely the secondary-school student will establish his or her expectations in light of what he or she hears from peers in those institutions. In that sense, community colleges, most state colleges, and local/regional private colleges have far more significant influence on the choices made by the average secondary-school student than do the elite private institutions or the flagship state universities . . . The message gets around, and, as I noted, the more local or regional the postsecondary institution, the faster the message moves into the high-school culture—and with greater force. (Adelman 1984)

The pervasive influence of college entry and exit requirements upon high schools places a heavy responsibility upon colleges and universities. *In far too many instances college-graduation requirements appear to represent a treaty drawn among warring nations rather than a rational, research-based program of study.* If you don't believe that, just try to remove a course from the required program of study for a college degree. You will hear much talk about wanting the best for students or wanting them to be liberally educated. But in many instances this rhetoric can be translated to "Don't touch my course because my enrollment depends on this requirement."

A recent newspaper account of a proposed change from institutional to department requirements in establishing graduation

113

requirements from the University of the District of Columbia, an open-admissions university, best illustrates this point:

> The University of the District of Columbia Faculty Senate voted yesterday to condemn recently proposed changes in graduation requirements for most students.
>
> In an emotionally charged meeting at the Northwest campus, several faculty members complained that the reputation of the institution and its students has been "damaged" by the proposal, recommended by UDC President Robert L. Green and given preliminary approval by the board of trustees . . . Some faculty members spoke for the proposal, saying each academic department would be able to establish its own standards under the plan. "What are you afraid of?" associate professor of computer science Carl Friedman asked his colleagues.
>
> "The bottom line is that we want to make sure our students are well equipped," said Johnson [Wilmer Johnson, Faculty Senate President], who was frequently cheered and applauded by senate members for his criticism of the proposal. "If there is a concern that all students learn something about computers, then add it to the requirements, don't displace something else that we feel is of value." (*Washington Post* 1985)

Someone should write a book about higher education entitled *Yes, But You Didn't Take My Class.* Each professor feels that his or her course is the most important and should be required.

It is now estimated that over seventy percent of all high-school graduates will eventually attend a postsecondary institution of one kind or another for one or more years. Our society and the economy are making a postsecondary degree the entry credential for a growing list of occupations. The associate degree is becoming the preferred credential for entry into many mid-level occupations. Furthermore, individuals see the completion of a postsecondary degree as a major avenue leading into the economic mainstream of American life. *Today, fifty-five percent of all entering college freshmen are beginning their college careers in a two-year college.* This fact alone should be enough to motivate program coordination between the high schools and the community colleges of the country.

Secondary schools prepare students for the next step, whatever that step may be. But the numbers would tell us that they prepare only some of the students for that next step. According to the National Center for Education Statistics, about twenty-seven percent of high-school students drop out before graduation, and there has been a five-percent increase in that percentage from 1972 to 1982. Of the number that do graduate from high school about one-half move immediately into some type of postsecondary education, but only twenty-six percent of that group complete a baccalaureate degree. (Plesko and Stern 1985) Within the educational program patterns of these students, there are worrisome indicators of slippage.

As I have noted, one area of concern for the high school should be the increasing number of students enrolled in the general curriculum. As a rule, these "general education" students receive less career counseling, have fewer marketable skills, and are unlikely to find the kinds of work that can be seen as an initial step up a career ladder, at least for several years. Their expectations are vague and unrealistic. The greatest single indicator of slippage is that nearly two out of three of the high-school dropouts indicate they were enrolled in the high-school general-education track at the time they left school. (Adelman 1983)

Some twenty-seven percent of high-school graduates finish vocational programs. But the percentage educated as technicians is very low (one percent). Almost fifty percent of high-school vocational training is in agriculture, home economics, and industrial arts, areas that do not reflect the most pressing needs of the marketplace. Nor do most high schools have the resources to mount sophisticated technical education programs that more nearly reflect the needs of the marketplace. As community colleges well know, such training programs are usually expensive and constantly in need of update.

If projections hold, between now and 1990 the percentage of students that finish baccalaureate degrees will remain relatively stable, but the percentage seeking further education and training beyond high school, particularly the associate degree, will continue to increase by an estimated ten percent. Generally speaking, those high-school students coming to community, technical, and junior colleges for further education and training will already be hampered by poor decisions and an unfocused high-school

115

general-education program unless high-school and community college leaders can provide the motivation for some intensive program coordination and lifting of student visions.

Nationally, community college retention figures hover at fifty percent. From semester to semester, only about half the students who enroll go on to complete the program. The reasons are numerous and complex, but the impact of this slippage upon individual lives is pervasive. A high-school general-education program, low high-school grades, and vague educational aspirations are important and possibly crucial factors in community, technical, and junior college withdrawals.

New and different curricular models must be designed to slow the slippage, to bring more structure and substance to the curricular program, and to make college-program and degree completion more likely for more students.

Factors in High-School/Community College Cooperation

In a recent American Association of Community and Junior Colleges survey of community, technical, and junior college administrators, an overwhelming majority reported some type of collaborative arrangements between their college and high schools, falling for the most part into the following four categories:

- Joint enrollment is the most common cooperative program. It provides a stimulating challenge for students who want more than the standard high school can offer. Some state-level funding formulas reward both schools and colleges for joint-enrollment participation. However, this type of cooperation should not be confused with truly collaborative efforts requiring commitments from the school and college. In these days of shrinking enrollments, the joint-enrollment program is viewed by some high-school personnel as a self-serving student-recruitment program on the part of the college.
- Sharing of faculty and/or facilities is another form of cooperation. High-school students may take classes in a nearby community college facility. The classes are taught by a community college faculty member. Although not as common, college faculty may go to the high school to teach a class.

This type of program requires cooperation, but little in the way of real program articulation or collaboration.

- Advanced placement is a program aimed at motivating academically gifted students to earn college credit while still in high school. Even though placement is primarily determined by tests, an increasing number of community colleges are offering advanced-placement credit. Again, little collaborative commitment is required from either the schools or colleges to establish or maintain this program.
- Program coordination efforts, though few and far between, are increasing. High schools and community colleges develop written program-articulation agreements. These agreements are most often found in vocational/technical courses and programs. This is the most important type of cooperation, but it is also the most difficult collaborative effort to sustain. Here are the most commonly cited issues that inhibit and discourage this type of cooperation:

1. *Turf*—The single most often cited problem is turf. Cooperative programming is viewed as an intrusion on one program or another. There is a reluctance by either institution to give up anything. Program articulation is viewed as a threat to programs.
2. *State Leadership*—There is a lack of sustained and vigorous state-level leadership to establish linkages between community colleges and high schools in most states, with little state-level encouragement and few rewards to promote articulation efforts. In fact, in some states there is less communication between secondary-school leaders and community college leaders at the state level than at the local level.
3. *Resources*—Inadequate funds and lack of staff time are often mentioned as problems to overcome. In addition, high-school personnel in particular fear articulation efforts may mean some loss of students and/or funds.
4. *Scheduling*—Different calendars and different time schedules appear to slow down some articulation efforts.
5. *Community College Image*—In the eyes of some high-school administrators and faculty, community college

117

programs have an "image" problem. There is nothing particularly unusual about this problem, since community colleges are so new upon the educational scene. Nevertheless, solving this problem does require careful thought from community college leaders. Image-building is a long and slow process requiring consistent and open communication.

6. *Lack of Communication*—Little communication among college and high-school officials, college and high-school trustees, is often cited as inhibiting collaborative programs. Baird Whitlock writes:

> The unwillingness on the part of many college faculty members to believe that secondary-school teachers can teach at the college level has not changed very much. Robert Frost once said that the basic difference in post-lecture parties he attended in Britain and America was that in Britain, along with the college faculty, local doctors, lawyers, clergy, and businessmen, there would always be secondary-school teachers; in America this latter group was almost never present. For easier articulation to take place for students, the inner wall of separation within the academic community must be broken down. The distrust will never melt away until genuine conversation between the two groups of teachers begins. (Whitlock 1978)

7. *Focus Upon Machinery Rather Than Action*—When the effort to establish collaborative programs is made, much time is wasted on insignificant matters. It is difficult to obtain action plans.

In order to ensure cooperation, college leaders will be required to develop a "let's work together" style of operation and address substantive issues like curriculum coordination, student retention, and real program coordination, rather than enrollment development and student recruitment:

> Time and time again, when people think about collaboration they focus first on budgets and bureaucracy, on the costs involved, on hiring one or two directors, on renting space, on paper clips and new letterhead.
> This is self-defeating. And quite frankly, this kind of talk is frequently a smokescreen for an unwillingness to act. While resources

are important, they should not become the preoccupation of school and college planners. The most successful programs are those for which people see a need and find time to act—with little red tape or extra funding. (Boyer 1983)

Collaboration and program articulation are not easy. Three out of four community, technical, and junior college leaders report their colleges are doing little or nothing in the areas of program coordination and articulation. This should surprise no one, given the few rewards and abundant frustrations leaders experience in attempting collaborative efforts. But there are a few keys and consistent patterns that can be observed in the successful programs.

- First and foremost, the policymakers (school boards and trustees) must make a policy demand upon the system that program coordination and articulation be the order of the day. Furthermore, they should meet jointly a couple of times a year to hear progress reports from the staff.
- The chief executive officers of the college and school systems must take the initial responsibility to begin the dialogue and maintain the communication. Only top-level leadership will sustain this kind of effort. In addition, these individuals will be giving clear signals to principals and faculty that this is an important and sustained effort.
- Early in the discussions, agreement should be reached on a program focus—a priority for action. The initial tendency is to take on too much; as a consequence, the discussions involve too many people and too many considerations, sinking of their own weight. Pick out one or two programs that look like winners. Take the easy ones first and demonstrate a winner or two right at the start.
- Participants should receive some recognition and rewards, including reduced work loads where possible. This is particularly important for those key instructors involved.
- One individual must be assigned to serve as executive secretary or executive director of the project. Someone must have the responsibility to build the agendas, call the meetings, maintain the action record of meetings, maintain a time-line schedule, and edit the reports.

119

- A specific charge of duties for the participants should be developed that outlines purpose, time-lines, and duties.
- Periodic progress reports are essential.
- The end product should be a written program-coordination agreement that is widely distributed among those who must carry the agreement into action.
- All agreements should be reviewed on an annual basis.

The good news is that several community, technical, and junior colleges have developed high-school/college partnerships and articulation efforts that eliminate much of the guesswork about what is expected of high-school students. A few of the partnerships and articulation programs are summarized here. This list is not intended to be exhaustive, but only representative of ongoing and increasing high-school/community college partnership efforts.

- LaGuardia Community College (a unit of the City University of New York) has established the Center for High-School/College Articulation, an information network to encourage the exchange of data on high-school/college programs. Under the leadership of college President Joe Shenker and Director Janet Lieberman, the Center recently published the first edition of the *Yellow Pages Directory*, a compilation of information on high-school/college articulation at both two-year and four-year institutions.
- LaGuardia and the New York City Board of Education also operate Middle College. Students enter in the eleventh grade and work toward a high-school diploma and an associate of liberal arts degree simultaneously. Both the high-school and college portions of the program are located on the community college campus. A special feature of the program requires that every student in Middle College spend a portion of the year in volunteer work in the community.
- Miami-Dade Community College has developed an exemplary cooperative effort with the Dade County Public Schools. Since the 1960's, high-school students have been enrolling in courses offered by the college and receiving both college and high-school credit. Florida law now allows both the high school and the community college to collect state funds for

a concurrently enrolled student. Miami-Dade Community College President Robert McCabe also serves as Chair of the Southeast Florida Educational Consortium involving the public and private schools and colleges of southeast Florida. This consortium has developed an outstanding publication entitled *Planning Your Education: A Guide to Getting the Most Out of High School*, distributed to every tenth-grader in the southeast Florida region.

- The Kern Community College System, Bakersfield College, and Kern High School District in California are developing a 2 + 2 (grades eleven through fourteen) tech-prep/associate degree in agriculture as a result of earlier successful efforts with this concept. This consortium of schools and colleges is also working to develop 2 + 2 curricula in English, math, humanities, and some technologies. An interesting aspect of this collaborative effort is the development of a competency certificate at the conclusion of each year of study.

- The Alamo Community College District and San Antonio College have established a high-technology high school, the only publicly funded school of its kind in Texas. Located on the college campus, the school enrolls junior- and senior-high-school students in science, math, and computer courses taught by college faculty. In addition to receiving credit toward high-school graduation, they also receive a special certificate from the high-tech high school. The school opened in the fall of 1983 with phase one, a baccalaureate-degree track that prepares students for college-level work through advanced courses. A technology-related track is scheduled to open in the fall of 1985.

- The Dallas County Community College District is cooperating with area school districts to develop a high-school/community college articulation plan in fourteen occupational programs. This articulation plan makes it possible to grant equivalent college credit for high-school mastery in these programs. All fourteen programs have manuals listing required competencies and the criteria for determining mastery. Student profile sheets are used to record mastery and as the basis for awarding equivalent college credit.

121

- Williamsport Area Community College in Pennsylvania has developed a program that allows eleventh and twelfth graders to enroll in college vocational/technical-education programs. Currently, approximately 800 high-school students are enrolled in fifteen specially designed programs.
- The Community College of Rhode Island has developed an excellent guide aimed at high-school freshmen indicating the kind of high-school preparation required to succeed in community college programs.
- Hudson County College has developed a joint enrollment program with the Jersey City Schools.
- Hagerstown Junior College in Maryland has initiated cooperative agreements with Washington County high schools. College credit is offered for advanced courses in biology, English, foreign languages, and secretarial sciences.
- The Florida State Board for Community Colleges has adopted a state-level rule that requires articulation agreements to be executed between local community college boards of trustees and local school district boards to enhance learning opportunities and avoid duplication of courses. The 1982 Master Plan for Florida Postsecondary Education states: "The sequence and continuity of a student's education are enhanced by the creation of a continuum based upon communication, smooth transition, cooperative and unified philosophy."

Here are a few tips for action that seem to smooth the road in helping the program-coordination efforts. Prior to initial program-discussion meetings, some analysis information should be prepared to help all participants begin the discussion with the same information base:

High School	Postsecondary
How are our college-prep/ baccalaureate-degree students doing in the college-transfer program?	How can we improve on the number of students completing an associate degree?
What are we doing for that fifty percent of the student	How can we provide associate-degree technicians to meet

High School	Postsecondary
population that is not pursuing an academic or vocational track?	future employer needs?
What are characteristics of the middle quartiles of the student body?	What are present and future technician job requirements? —numbers —competencies —experience
What are the expectations of students beyond high school? —capabilities —motivation	What kinds of "clear signals" are given high-school students about program entry and exit requirements?
What curriculum are students completing in high school?	What curriculum changes are needed in community college programs?
What are recent students doing after graduation?	Can the community college adequately respond to required changes? —time (are two years enough?) — resources (teachers, equipment) — capability of students
How can students be given more structure and more substance in their school program?	What kind of feedback information is the community college giving the high schools about student performance in the liberal arts and fine arts as well as the practical arts programs?

Some of the program coordination issues to be discussed in articulation meetings include:

- Analysis of the common core of learning required for various programs.

123

- Jobs Analysis—Which jobs require preparation beyond high school?
- Curriculum Analysis—What should be taught? Who determines what course content?
- Turf Analysis—Which institution should offer a particular course?
- Credit Analysis—What determines satisfactory completion of a course?
- Facilities Analysis—Where should a course be taught?
- Faculty Analysis—Who should teach a particular course? Why?
- Involvements Analysis—Should co-op training be included?
- Competencies Analysis—What competencies can be identified as program requirements? Should competency certificates be issued? If so, when?
- Evaluation Analysis—Who measures the effectiveness of the coordinated program?
- Student Analysis—Do wide variances in abilities require the development of multiple teaching-learning approaches?
- Development of a Written Agreement—How often should the coordination agreement be reviewed and revised?

Figure 17

Sample Coordination Structure

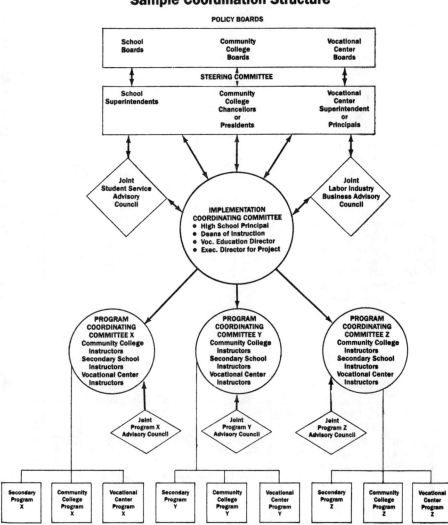

Figure 18

Sample Time Line

Meetings	Months							
1. Meetings of Policy Boards to establish policy demand upon the various systems and hear progress reports.	▶							▶
2. Meetings of the Steering Committee to establish the operational procedures, establish program priorities, appoint the Implementation Coordination Committee, and review progress.			▶	▶	▶	▶	▶	
3. Meetings of the Implementation Coordination Committee to appoint Program Coordinating Committees, meet with the Joint Labor Industry, Business Advisory Council, and operationalize the program.			▶	▶	▶	▶	▶	▶
4. Meetings of the Program Coordinating Committees to discuss, develop, and agree upon program specifics.				▶	▶	▶	▶	
5. Meetings of the Joint Student Services Advisory Council.				▶		▶		▶
6. Meetings of the Joint Labor, Industry, Business, Education Advisory Council.		▶						▶

126

STEERING COMMITTEE

Description: Chief executive officer from each participating institution

Purpose: Set operating procedures, establish priorities, appoint implementation committees, approve coordination agreement, secure resources

Meet: Every other month (5 or 6 times a year)

Responsibilities:

- Approve tentative program priorities (pick program)
- Assign representatives to implementation committee
- Involve/encourage institutional participation
- Obtain resources for program implementation at institution
- Appoint representatives to joint labor, industry, business, education advisory council and joint student services advisory council

Representatives:

_____

_____

_____

_____

_____

_____

_____

IMPLEMENTATION COMMITTEE

Description: Administrator from each participating institution as assigned by the institutional executive

Purpose: Develop guidelines, procedures, and cooperative agreements for coordinated programs: assign committee representatives and direct activities at respective institutions

Meet: Monthly, continuing as programs are implemented

Responsibilities:

- Appoint program coordinating committees
- Identify/resolve administrative coordination issues
- Develop procedure for implementing plans
- Draft final agreements and program proposals
- Establish institutional budgets, personnel and facilities requirements for program participation
- Meet with advisory committees

Representatives:

_____

127

_____

_____

_____

_____

_____

_____

_____

- Review needs as expressed by advisory personnel
- Identify/address curriculum issues for coordination
- Identify where/who will teach various courses and labs in coordination program
- Establish proficiency levels for competency certificates
- Establish program review process
- Identify/address curriculum issues for coordination

PROGRAM COORDINATING COMMITTEE

Description: Program specialists/ faculty/staff

Purpose: Identify and address curriculum and implementation issues

Meet: Monthly

Responsibilities:

- Review curriculum for all involved institutions

Membership:

_____

_____

_____

_____

_____

_____

Some Initial Agenda Items for Program Coordinating Committees

A. List courses currently offered at the postsecondary level that are very similar to courses offered at the secondary school and vice versa. (These courses are the ones that are highly desirable for coordination.)

Course Name

Name of the Secondary or Postsecondary School Offering the Course

1. _____   _____

2. _____   _____

3. _____   _____

4. _____   _____

B. List courses currently offered at the postsecondary level that you believe could be but are not currently offered at the secondary school and vice versa. (These courses are potentially suitable for coordination.)

1. _____ _____

2. _____ _____

3. _____ _____

4. _____ _____

C. For each course listed above, identify the postsecondary school curriculum or curriculums of which each course is a part. (Doing this will help visualize the impact of coordination.)

1. _____ _____

2. _____ _____

3. _____ _____

4. _____ _____

D. List the state-level, community personnel and agencies that should be contacted for information or help in these discussions:

Name: _____ Agency: _____

Title: _____ Address: _____

Phone: _____

Name: _____ Agency: _____

Title: _____ Address: _____

Phone: _____

Name: _____ Agency: _____

Title: _____ Address: _____

Phone: _____

- Is there institutional commitment from top to bottom for program coordination in this program?
- How are the various coordinating committees working?
- Has a written program coordination agreement been developed?
- Do state-level personnel and advisory personnel support the agreement?
- What do periodic evaluations reveal?
- Are students well served?

Chapter VII

The 2+2 Tech-Prep/ Associate-Degree Program: Making Winners of Ordinary Students

. . . there is surprisingly little attention given to "ordinary people" in the school reform reports. There is the clear implication that the rising tide of mediocrity is made up of an embarrassing number of ordinary people, and if we want to return excellence to education, we better go out and find more excellent people.

K. Patricia Cross, Harvard Graduate School of Education

T he heart of the message we have heard from parents, students, politicians, and policymakers is this: *Give us more structure; give us more substance in our educational programs. Help us develop the confidence that the materials and scaffolding of our educational structures match the real-life needs of all our students.*

One of the most recent reform reports points a finger of guilt at the colleges and universities for some of the breakdown in educational-program structure and substance. A distinguished panel of higher-education leaders forthrightly states the problem:

> As for what passes as a college curriculum, almost anything goes. We have reached a point at which we are more confident about the length of a college education than its content and purpose ... Electives are being used to fatten majors and diminish breadth. It is as if no one cared, so long as the store stays open.
>
> One consequence of the abandonment of structure by the colleges has been the abandonment of structure in the schools. The decline in requirements is contagious, and in the absence of system in national educational arrangements, articulation between secondary and higher education has been allowed to break down. The result is a loss of rigor both in the secondary and in the collegiate course of study. That loss of definition and rigor has encouraged the false notion that there is such a thing as effortless learning, a notion that finds expression in curricular practice and student behavior. As the colleges have lost a firm grasp on their goals and mission, so have the secondary schools. (Association of American Colleges 1985)

The requirements listed for most college degrees look more like a treaty among warring nations than a coherent vision of what it means to be an educated person.

In many ways the associate degree is aimed at maintaining community college comprehensiveness and seeking balance in the curriculum. The associate degree is not only central to the mission of the community, technical, and junior college, but it is also a quality-control issue. Colleges have suffered unintended negative public relations from well-meaning but semi-literate individuals who take a college class or two and then go to the university or to an employer and say, "I am a student of the Community College."

We simply cannot allow the debate about the importance of the liberal arts and the practical arts to degenerate into an either/ or argument. They are both important and balance is needed. Educational excellence must be defined in terms of connectedness and applicability, particularly for that sixty to seventy percent of the population who do not work as well, nor as effectively, when dealing only with the abstract. The liberal arts and the practical arts absolutely need each other.

Students in vocational-technical education programs must meet the same basic skill requirements as any other student seeking the high school diploma. But, it must be quickly pointed out that a course in business-letter writing can be rigorous and help students demonstrate writing skills. A course in business mathematics can also be rigorous and help students master computing percentages or applying statistical methods. An applied-physics course can be rigorous and help students master essential academic knowledge through practical experiences. Balance, connectedness, and continuity are key words in any reshaping of the curriculum aimed at improving the education of the middle quartile of students.

Research and experience tell us that students work better with goals; indeed, so do we all. Yet there is a lack of clarity in what high schools and postsecondary institutions expect of their students. Furthermore, there is poor communication between these two educational entities. Even more serious, there is a subtle but stubborn provincialism that suggests that program *articulation*, the careful building of bridges between high schools and colleges, and program *evaluation*, the careful measure of program success or failure, are extraneous to the primary mission of either group.

The national reports have given only cursory attention to the need for continuity in learning, forgetting all the dangerous lessons that the business world has learned of late—what happens when the left hand does not really understand what the right is about? The indicators are not difficult to find.

The concern that high-school students are still not concentrating on developing the "new basics" has been confirmed in a study by the National Center for Education Statistics. The study found that students are not taking recommended loads in such basic subjects as mathematics, science, and computer science. Interestingly, in the twelfth grade, the senior year, fewer courses were completed in these targeted areas than in any other high-school year, even though these seniors were below recommended program guidelines.

High schools generally do not have a good sense of how their students perform once at college or in the work world, as the colleges and universities, with rare exception, do not keep them informed. Community colleges, who often must deal with students who have failed to reach their own or others' expectations upon high-school graduation, are particularly lax in letting high schools know how their former students are doing.

Generally speaking, although the high-school courses a student takes do not seem important in getting him or her into a community college, they may be absolutely critical to success once the student is there. Yet, there is precious little communication to high-school students from the community, technical, and junior colleges about college *exit* requirements and the recommended high-school preparation related to these exit and program-completion requirements.

In *The Third Wave* Alvin Toffler describes our future world in terms of waves of change. The first wave of change was the agricultural revolution, which took a thousand years to develop. The second wave brought on the industrial revolution, over a mere 300 years. A technology-driven third wave is sweeping the world in a few decades and affecting almost every aspect of our lives. Robots are invading our factories. Electronic mail is becoming a standard communication device. Disease detection and prevention have been greatly improved. Superspeed air travel is now commonplace. The videocassette recorder is becoming a part of the home entertainment center and was the hottest

Christmas sales item of 1984. Laser technology, genetic engineering, and computer literacy are becoming common phrases in everyday communications. Odetics, Inc., a southern California high-technology firm, has just announced the development of Odex II, a computerized mobile robot, both agile and strong. It is not only capable of climbing on the back of a pickup truck, but is also capable of lifting the truck. This six-legged wonder can tackle jobs in such high-risk areas as nuclear power plants, stifling mine shafts, or burning buildings. In the initial development and production phase of this robot many engineers and scientists are required. But when 50,000 of these robots are being produced a year, the commercialization of technology will require many technicians for the manufacture, operation, programming, and repair of these machines.

Research on the organic computer, or "biochip," is a growing priority for some genetic engineers, chemists, mathematicians, and molecular biologists. Can we grow computer circuitry in biology labs from living bacteria producing powerful microprocessors? If it can be done, future computer circuits will be designed from groups of organic proteins the size of molecules that will serve as microscopic memory and switching devices, with the ability to more or less assemble themselves.

The Office of Technology Assessment serving the Congress of the United States lists communities across the country that are considered "hotbeds" of technology development: Huntsville, Alabama; Phoenix, Arizona; San Diego, California; Los Angeles, California; Santa Clara County, California; Colorado Springs, Colorado; Brevard County, Florida; Orlando, Florida; Chicago, Illinois; Montgomery County, Maryland; Lowell, Massachusetts; Minneapolis-St. Paul, Minnesota; Albuquerque, New Mexico; Portland, Oregon; Philadelphia, Pennsylvania; Oak Ridge, Tennessee; Austin, Texas; San Antonio, Texas; Salt Lake City, Utah; Burlington, Vermont; Seattle, Washington; Milwaukee, Wisconsin. Futurists tend to agree that the next twenty to thirty years will be a time of explosive progress. Robert Weinstein states:

> Like it or not, our educational institutions have little choice but
> to change with the times. Either that or be left in the wake of

136

untold technological breakthroughs. Many schools obstinately cling to the past, while others are busy designing curriculums to meet the needs of tomorrow. Yet, it's only a matter of time before even the most reactionary open themselves up to what lies ahead. If our educational system can no longer train and educate our young for the jobs of tomorrow, education has little relevancy. (Weinstein 1983)

Training and education have become integral to most broad-technology workers whether they be nurses, law-enforcement officers, electronic technicians, aircraft technicians, computer operators, auto-service personnel, or marketing representatives. IBM now requires each technician, marketing representative, and systems analyst in that large corporation to spend nineteen to twenty days (one working month) in education and training programs. And IBM is not alone in requiring such programs of its employees. Such widely diverse companies as State Farm Insurance, Southwest Forest Industries, Manufacturers Hanover Trust Company, Abbott Laboratories, Central Illinois Light Company, Citicorp, Steelcase Inc., Valley National Bank of Arizona, and Caterpillar Tractor Company all are moving education and training programs into high-priority positions in terms of strategic planning for economic growth. California Superintendent of Public Instruction Bill Honig has summed up the challenge for schools and colleges this way: "Don't be misled by advocates of a low-tech future. These modern Luddites have historically underestimated the extent and pace of change in the economy. They cite only a portion of the data from the Department of Labor, neglecting statistics that demonstrate substantive growth in jobs requiring high levels of preparation. They are out of step with the people who are hiring our graduates." (1985)

It is estimated that thirty billion dollars is spent annually by U.S. public and private employers for employee education and training programs. This figure does not include costs for training in the military. The Department of Defense estimates that some fifty billion dollars is spent on education and training per year when all DOD education and training costs are included. Public and private employers are concluding that the competencies and

137

related performance of the work force are the major factor in determining the economic and social health of their enterprise.

Clearly, more and more secondary schools and community colleges are waking up to the reality of shifting the curriculum to match a technological world:

> The growing pervasiveness of technology—and the certitude of ongoing technical advances—demands that we provide our young people with the solid base of scientific knowledge they will require. It is not only those who create technology who should have a competency in math and science. Those who use technology should also have a degree of understanding about the tools they use. They must also be able to adapt to changes in technology and the new skill requirements they bring with them. (Young 1985)

It is absolutely imperative that high schools and colleges, particularly community, technical, and junior colleges, become aggressive in examining, developing, and sustaining quality educational programs to serve that great host of Americans who keep this country working.

> *Who will keep our airplanes flying—*
> *our water flowing—*
> *our electricity charging—*
> *our hospitals operating—*
> *our trains tracking—*
> *our computers clicking—*
> *our cars running—*
> *our laws enforced—*
> *our goods and services sold—*

in a society saturated at every level with technology and information? I breathe a little prayer each time I climb on an airplane: Dear Lord, I just pray that the air-frame and power-plant technicians that serviced this plane had excellent education and training programs—and that they enjoy their work!

> Today, graduating high-school seniors can either go right to work, pursue a formal college education, or attend technical school or junior college. In the future we can look forward to new options. Community colleges, for one, will have a lot more credibility than

they have today. Although they will still be regarded as interim programs for those unsure of what they want to do with their lives, the community colleges of the future will work closely with the community and industry, thus having a much stronger identity. Industry leaders and teaching staffs will put their heads together to devise curriculums that provide real jobs for graduating seniors . . . For a growing number of young people, a two-year associate degree or possibly a company- or union-sponsored training program makes more sense. (Weinstein 1983)

The prediction that community colleges of the future will work closely with employers has already come true. *Three out of four community, technical, and junior colleges now report their participation in one or more employer/college partnership arrangements.* Has the time arrived to take the next step in establishing formal community college program partnerships with high schools? How about establishing a new four-year tech-prep/associate-degree program of cooperation between high schools and community, technical, and junior colleges?

Many academically talented secondary-school students have been well served over the years by the college-prep/baccalaureate-degree program, and that work must continue with even greater vigor and attention. But the ordinary students, the middle fifty percent of the high-school student population, have not been served so well. Some eleven million students out of the forty million now enrolled in elementary and secondary schools will not even graduate from high school. Many of these drop-outs will find their way to the community college within a few years without the requisite preparatory background.

It should be underlined at this point that the college-prep/baccalaureate-degree program remains one of the priority programs for the community college. More and more recent high-school graduates are experiencing a cost-effective and excellent undergraduate two years in a community college. *In case study after case study students report they experienced the best teaching of their college careers in the community college.* More students must be encouraged to continue on through the community college and to complete the baccalaureate-degree program. Community colleges are working diligently and must continue to do so to provide a first-rate program leading to the baccalaureate degree. But the traditional college-prep/baccalaureate-degree program is not the focus of this book, even though it remains a top priority in the work of the community college.

Assumptions of the Tech-Prep/Associate-Degree Program

The tech-prep/associate-degree program advocates taking a step beyond the current and usually cosmetic high-school/college partnership arrangements into *substantive* program coordination. The program seeks a middle ground that blends the liberal arts with the practical arts without diluting the time-honored baccalaureate-degree/college-prep track. A closely coordinated four-year (grades eleven through fourteen) liberal-technical education program will provide more room for an electives program than can be achieved in two unconnected years.

The program targets are (1) the middle quartiles of the typical high-school student body in terms of academic talent and interest, and (2) the mid-range of occupations requiring some beyond-high-school education and training but not necessarily a baccalaureate degree. The tech-prep/associate-degree program rests on the following assumptions:

1. Additional program structure and substance are required for most high-school students.
2. Continuity in learning is an important and often vital ingredient for student success.
3. Community, technical, and junior colleges have generally failed to give clear signals to high-school students and their parents about what constitutes an exemplary high-school preparatory program, particularly to those students headed for technical-education programs.
4. The most growth over the next fifteen years will occur in those occupations requiring some postsecondary education and training but less than a baccalaureate degree. Professional and technical workers are expected to replace clerical workers as the largest occupational group. (Pyatt 1985)
5. Most of the emerging (and some of the older) technical-education programs cannot be completed adequately in

two years, particularly if the student has had inadequate secondary-school preparation. Excellent liberal/technical-education programs require more time. Furthermore, high schools report little technical education is going on at that level.

6. The junior and senior years of high school can be better utilized by many students. The senior year in particular has sometimes been seen as a waste of time for some students.

7. The current twenty-seven-percent high-school drop-out rate can be reduced if students understand the "why" of their learning as well as the "how." This means a breaking down of the walls between vocational and academic education. The largest volume of dropping out of high school occurs between grades ten and eleven. This volume can be reduced if students see a focused alternative-learning program that connects the curriculum with real-life issues.

8. Focused learning motivates more students than does unfocused learning.

9. The associate degree is becoming an increasingly preferred degree by employers for entry into many mid-level occupations.

10. Secondary schools must be preparatory institutions for *all* students and not just for college-prep/baccalaureate-degree-bound students. Students must be better prepared to take that next step, whatever that step may be.

11. Standards of excellence must be developed for all programs, particularly for the middle quartiles of students.

12. Guidance programs must present all high-school students with a curricular program whose goals are clear. The guidance program must also be prepared to help students shift their goals from time to time. Aimlessness is one of the plagues of secondary-school and college students: goals must remain within clear vision of the student.

13. High-school and college faculty and administrators can coordinate their programs and can communicate more effectively when a clear signal is given from the policy-makers that there is a policy demand upon the system.

14. Neither the current college-prep/baccalaureate-degree track nor the traditional vocational-education job-specific track will adequately serve the needs of a majority of the students in the future, while a general-education track serves the needs of none. Placing all students in a theory-based baccalaureate-degree program, as recommended in so many of the reform reports, fails to recognize the tremendous individual differences in student abilities, aptitudes, learning speeds and styles, and backgrounds.

Here are some facts to ponder when considering the tech-prep/associate-degree program:

- Fifty-five percent of entering freshmen in all of higher education now begin their college careers in community, technical, or junior colleges.
- Eighty-three percent of the current adult population do not hold bachelor degrees.
- Twenty-seven percent, or one out of four students, do not complete high school. This means that some ten to eleven million will not complete a high-school program unless changes are forthcoming.
- As reported by the high-school graduates in the National Longitudinal Study of the class of 1980, programs of study completed were

Academic (college prep)	- 37%
Vocational	- 19%
General	- 42%
Unreported	- 2%

- Nearly two-thirds of the high-school drop-outs come from the general-education program.
- The Southern Regional Education Board reports that fewer than one percent of the high-school students in vocational programs are involved in technical-education programs. To remedy this situation, the SREB advocates that high schools, postsecondary institutions, and employers together should develop 2 + 2 programs in which a planned four-year curriculum connects the last two years of high school with two

years of postsecondary study along with planned, on-the-job learning. The planned curriculum would include both academic and technical courses.

- The American Electronic Association report entitled "Technical Employment Projects, 1983-87" indicates that the electronic industry will need sixty percent more technicians by 1987 than were employed in 1983. That means 115,000 new electronic technician jobs will be needed by 1987, in addition to other worker replacements.
- The twenty fastest-growing occupations in 1982-1995 all prefer postsecondary education and training, e.g., computer science technician, office machine service technician, engineering technician, banking and insurance personnel. Only two of the twenty require a baccalaureate degree for entry.
- Private-sector employment growth in the future will be in companies with fifty or fewer employees.
- The associate degree is becoming the preferred degree for entry into many technician occupations.
- American private-sector business and industry spend an estimated thirty billion dollars a year on the education and training of eleven million employees.
- All who will be in the work force by the year 2000 are alive today.
- A recent Penn State University study indicates that ninety percent of entering college students in 1982 and 1983 expect a B average in college. Sixty-one percent estimated they would study fewer than twenty hours per week.
- The same Penn State study found that eighty percent of entering college students said they knew little or nothing about their choice of major.

The Tech-Prep/Associate-Degree Program: A Liberal-Technical Education

The four-year 2 + 2 tech-prep/associate-degree program is intended to run parallel with and not replace the current college-prep/baccalaureate-degree program. It will combine a common core of learning and technical education and will rest upon a foundation of basic proficiency development in math, science, communications, and technology—all in an applied setting, but with the tests of excellence applied to these programs as well as others.

Beginning with the junior year in high school, students will select the tech-prep program (even as they now select the college-prep program) and continue for four years in a structured and closely coordinated high-school/college curriculum. They will be taught by high-school teachers in the first two years, but will also have access to college personnel and facilities when appropriate. Starting with a solid base of applied science, applied math, literacy courses, and technical programs, the high-school portion of the career program will be intentionally preparatory in nature. Built around career clusters and technical-systems study, such a tech-prep approach will help students develop broad-based competence in a career field and avoid the pitfalls of more short-term and narrowly delineated job training. *It is the responsibility of the high school to open up the world for the high-school student rather than close it down through narrow and specific job training.*

Based upon locally developed agreements, the tech-prep/associate-degree program can be developed with many options for the student. The high-school experience can be primarily in the liberal arts, leaving the technical education for the postsecondary school years. The reverse of this pattern can also be developed, depending upon high-school equipment and facilities. The usual scope and sequence of the tech-prep/associate-degree program would indicate leaving the highly specific areas of the technical-education program for the latter two years. However, it is not so important where, or even when, the student gains the required learning. What is important is that the student see the program spelled out and see the "gestalt" of the entire four years.

This high-school tech-prep program must dovetail with specific technical education programs on the postsecondary level. More intense technical specialization will be developed at the college level, always in tandem with broad technical competence and broad educational competence aimed at working in a wide-technology society. The community college technical-education programs include law enforcement, nursing, electronics, computers, business, marketing, entrepreneurship, agriculture, electron microscopy, construction trades (usually in cooperation with the apprenticeship program), mechanical technologies, and many others.

It is anticipated that one result of this program will be the enhancement of the associate degree so that it will become the preferred degree for employers seeking to fill a broad range of mid-level occupations. As a result of employer demand, many students are now seeking the associate degree as a preferred career development goal. Over 400,000 of these degrees were awarded in 1984 and the trend is upward.

Making the Partnership Work

The tech-prep/associate-degree program will require close curricular coordination. Most of all, it will require high-school and community college leaders and faculty members to talk regularly with one another and with employers.

The tech-prep/associate-degree concept provides a dramatic model for educators wishing to avoid slippage and loss of continuity in learning. Most important, it brings program structure and substance to the ordinary student.

- Students will develop sound basic skills and knowledge.
- Students will obtain first-rate technical-education preparation.
- High schools will motivate more students and perhaps lose fewer students between grades ten and eleven because they can see a future—a "why" for their efforts.
- Colleges will gain better-prepared high-school graduates.
- The tech-prep/associate-degree program will encourage more high-school students to continue their education in meaningful ways.
- Employers will gain better prepared employees to work in a wide-technology society.

The history of cooperative and coordinated program articulation between high schools and community colleges would not even fill a slim book. But there are signs that progress is being made. The National Commission on Secondary Vocational Edu-

145

Figure 19

The Current Typical Comprehensive High-School Program Enrollment

College-Prep/Baccalaureate Degree Program	General Education Program	Vocational Education Program
37% of the students	42% of the students	19% of the students

cation gives its stamp of approval to the tech-prep/associate-degree program:

> Secondary and postsecondary levels must also coordinate their programs. The "tech-prep" curriculum being developed in some communities between high schools and community colleges illustrates how this can be done effectively. The program is solidly based in applied sciences, applied math, literacy courses, and technical programs. The high-school vocational-education part of the program covers career clusters and systems—electrical, fluid power, business, and mechanical. Study in such clusters and systems eases the transition to technical education programs in community colleges and other postsecondary institutions. (National Commission on Secondary Vocational Education 1984)

It must be understood by all concerned that the tech-prep/associate degree is flexible enough to meet the needs of a great diversity of human talent. There can be many options for students within this program depending upon student strengths and

Figure 20

The Future Typical Comprehensive High-School Program Enrollment

College-Prep/Baccalaureate Degree Program	Tech-Prep/Associate Degree Program	Vocational Education/ High School Diploma Program
⅓ of the high school student body	⅓ of the high school student body	⅓ of the high school student body

The number of students choosing each major will vary greatly from high school to high school and a common core of learning must undergird all programs.

weaknesses, faculty expertise, and the facilities of the participating institutions. Following are some options:

Figure 21

Tech-Prep/Associate-Degree Options

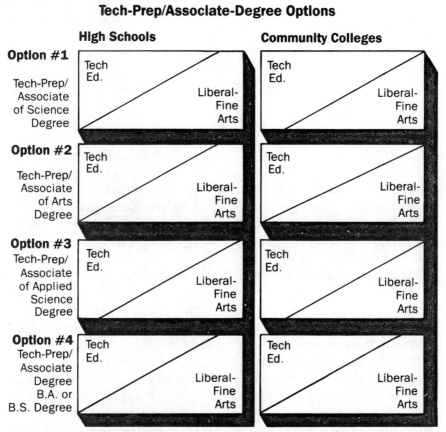

A major challenge for the tech-prep/associate-degree program
is the development of a rigorous program in applied science and
math. In this regard the State Directors of Vocational Education,
representing some thirty-two states, retained the Center for
Occupational Research Development in Waco, Texas, under the
leadership of Dan Hull, and the Agency for Instructional Technology, under the leadership of Bennie Lucroy, to develop a new
high-school applied-physics course called Principles of Technology. The goals of this course are to help students learn technical
principles and concepts, improve science and mathematics skills

and knowledge, and provide hands-on laboratory experience for technicians. Principles of Technology is now being field-tested in classrooms across America and will be available for general use in the 1985-86 school year. Video tapes and instructional manuals are being prepared to supplement the instructional materials to be utilized in 169 classes per year over the two years of grades eleven and twelve. Fourteen units of study form the foundation for the course, each focusing upon the scientific principles that are the foundation of today's technological developments:

1. Force
2. Work
3. Rate
4. Resistance
5. Energy
6. Power
7. Force Transformers
8. Momentum
9. Energy Converter
10. Optical Systems
11. Transducers
12. Time Constants
13. Vibrations
14. Radiation

These units deal with these principles as they apply to mechanical systems, fluid systems, thermal systems, and electrical systems.

The Principles of Technology course of study is an applied-physics course based upon the time-honored principles of physics but dressed in the clothes of modern technology. After viewing several of the video lessons, this writer has concluded that this is an information-rich and an experience-rich science curriculum which will motivate ordinary students to learn more physics than they might learn in a traditional theoretical-physics course of study. *The curriculum of the future must so integrate the instructional program that students can easily connect what they are learning with real-life issues.*

In general, though, change comes slowly to a school or college curriculum. If you don't believe that, ask John Saxon, math-textbook author and junior college math professor. His request for space to continue advertising his new algebra textbook was refused by *The Mathematics Teacher*, a journal for math teachers, because the editor thought his advertising had become too inflammatory. The state textbook commission refused to approve his algebra textbook despite enthusiastic praise from math teachers such as Barbara Stross, a Portland, Oregon, high-school math teacher, who states about the Saxon approach: "This is what teachers dream about . . . It's a combination of measurable academic achievement and a blossoming of confidence, pleasure and excitement in learning and practicing math." (Armbrister 1985)

Saxon's theory is simple. He is convinced that ordinary students not only can learn complicated mathematics, they can also enjoy it; math anxiety is produced by textbooks that are too stilted and too theoretical. Essentially the Saxon math-teaching approach focuses on practice and repetition while it helps students understand the "why" of their learning. According to Saxon, "Algebra is a skill like playing the piano . . . you do not teach a child the piano by teaching him music theory. Van Cliburn and Vladimir Horowitz practice. This is the way skills are mastered." (Armbrister 1985)

After some fourteen years of pushing and crusading, the Saxon algebra textbook is becoming widely used in junior and senior high schools across the country and ordinary students are learning algebra.

Jaime Escalante, a Bolivian immigrant who came to the United States twenty-one years ago unable to speak English, was honored at the 1985 convention of the American Association of Community and Junior Colleges as the distinguished faculty member of the year. Escalante completed an associate degree in electronics technology and a bachelor's degree in mathematics in order to pursue his first love—teaching. He chooses to work in a joint-appointment teaching assignment between the inner-city Garfield High School and East Los Angeles College.

Escalante's goal is to make math winners out of ordinary students, and his students have experienced extraordinary success in the advanced placement calculus examination. Sixty-three of his high-school math students received advanced placement credit in 1984. He anticipates that more than one hundred will receive college credit in 1985. This success is so astounding that the Educational Testing Service retested several of the students; the results were the same.

John Saxon and Jaime Escalante are symbolic of many other teachers in America who are proving on a day-to-day basis that ordinary students can experience excellence in learning as long as they are taught by those who understand one important concept: "Education has two roles. Its first is to prepare our young to be productive members of society. That means skill training and preparing people for the jobs of the future. Education's second purpose is more general, and that is to prepare young people—regardless of their eventual career choices—to understand the society in which they live." (Young 1985)

Meeting the Nation's Career Needs

The following lists reflect a growing trend in America today: the increasing number of occupations that require more than four years of high-school training but less than a baccalaureate degree. Those high schools and colleges which have articulated programs are best suited to meet the needs of America's work force, both now and for the future.

Some Occupations Related to the Physical Sciences

High-school graduation usually necessary or recommended	Two years of college or apprenticeship or specialized school usually necessary or recommended	Four or more years of college usually necessary or recommended
Construction helper	Aviation inspector	Aerospace engineer
Construction laborer	Aerospace technician	Anesthesiologist
Cook	Airborne and power	Anthropologist
Electrotyper and	plant technician	Archaeologist
stenotyper	Brick mason	Astronomer
Electroplater	Broadcast technician	Astrophysicist
Electronic assembler	Carpenter and contractor	Biochemist
Guard	Computer programmer	Cartographer
Janitor and custodian	Computer operator	Chemist
Laundry and dry-cleaning	Chef	Civil engineer
operator	Drafter	Computer engineer
Machine operator	Engineering technician	Electrical engineer
Truck driver	Electrician	Environmental
	Electronic technician	scientist
	Electron microscopist	Food and drug
	Graphic artist	analyst
	technician	Geographer
	Heating and air-	Geologist
	conditioning	Geophysicist
	technician	Industrial engineer
	Inspector	Mechanical
	Instrument and	engineer
	appliance repair	Metallurgical
	technician	engineer

150

Law technician
Law enforcer
Machinist
Millwright
Nuclear technician
Plumber and pipefitter
Quality control
    technician
Robotics technician
Sheet metal technician
Science technician
Tool and die maker
Travel agent
Systems analyst
Welding technician

Meteorologist
Nuclear engineer
Petroleum
    engineer
Pharmacologist
Physicist
Quality control
    engineer
Safety engineer
Traffic engineer

Some Occupations Related to the Life Sciences

Animal caretaker
Custodian
Dog trainer
Farmer
Florist
Gardener
Gamekeeper
Groundskeeper
Hunting and fishing
    guide
Lab assistant
Medical secretary
Museum worker
Nurse, aide
Nursery manager
Orchardist
Orderly
Recreation worker
Taxidermist
Waiter and waitress

Agricultural technician
Agricultural business-
    person
Biomedical equipment
    technician
Cytotechnologist
Dental ceramist
Dental hygienist
Dental lab technician
EEG technician
Electrologist
Fingerprint classifier
Fish and game warden
Food service supervisor
Forestry technician
Greenskeeper
    technician
Health inspector
Histologic technician
Inhalation therapist
Medical lab worker
Mortician
Nurse, assoc. degree R.N.
Nurse, practical
Ornamental horti-
    culture technician
Occupational therapist
    assistant
Paramedic
Radiologic technologist
Respiratory therapy
    technician
Recreation assistant
Water and waste
    treatment technician

Agronomist
Anthropologist
Athletic trainer
Audiologist
Bacteriologist
Biologist
Botanist
Curator
Dentist
Dietician
Entomologist
Food and drug
    inspector
Forester
Health educator
Horticulturist
Industrial
    hygienist
Landscape archi-
    tect
Medical librarian
Microbiologist
Nurse, B.A.
Occupational
    therapist
Optometrist
Physical therapist
Physician
Podiatrist
Psychologist
Public health
    officer
Recreation
    director
Taxonomist
Sanitarian
Teacher/professor
Veterinarian
Zoologist

151

These ten mythical help-wanted ads typify the shifts that futurists predict for the nation's job market, changes that are bound to affect the education and training of the work force of the future.

Geriatric Social Worker: Inner-city private nursing home, immediate opening for capable, reliable person. Must be L.P.N. or have equivalent education. Salary $16,000 to $22,000 depending on experience. References required. Equal Opportunity Employer. Associate degree preferred with broad education background.

Laser Process Technician: High-technology firm needs dependable, experienced laser technician. Should have two years related laser cutting machine experience or will train. Flex time and day care available. Job sharing and shared dividends. Salary $16,000 to $25,000 negotiable. E.O.E. Associate degree preferred with solid math and science background.

Genetic Engineering Technician: Positions available for both process technicians and engineering technicians. Relocation. Must have two years technical education and training. Additional education paid by company. Moving expenses paid by firm. Company will buy your present home. Salary $20,000 to $30,000. E.O.E. Associate degree preferred with broad science background.

Battery Technician: Large oil firm needs five technicians with previous experience in fuel cells or high-energy batteries. Shift work, O.T. available, dressing rooms and private locker, discount on all corporate products. Education and managerial training available. $15,000 to $20,000. E.O.E. Associate degree preferred.

Staff Assistant: County tax assessor needs dependable executive secretary skilled in use of word processor and microcomputer. Must have good interpersonal skills with ability to remain calm in conflict situations. Salary range: $16,000 to $24,000. E.O.E. Associate degree preferred with broad educational background.

Electronic Technicians: Small electronics company needs dependable and broadly educated technician. Must be knowledgeable of fluid power systems, mechanical systems, as well as electrical systems. Flex time available. Company stock plan available. Salary $18,000 to $28,000, negotiable. E.O.E. Associate degree preferred.

Police Officer: City of Serenity needs police officer who has completed an associate degree law enforcement training program or is graduate of a police academy. Excellent communication skills required. Preference in point system will be given to those candidates able to communicate in Spanish. Salary $20,000 to $30,000 with excellent fringe package. E.O.E.

Nurse: General Hospital needs dependable registered nurse for alternating shift work. Must have good interpersonal skills as well as technical nursing competencies. Salary range $18,000 to $25,000 with excellent fringe benefits package. E.O.E. Associate degree preferred.

Marketing Representative: Small computer-related firm needs dependable individual with sales education and training or equivalent experience. Must be knowledgeable of computer systems and electronics. Some on-the-job education and managerial training available. Associate degree preferred. Salary begins at $18,000 with additional commission based on sales volume. E.O.E.

Bookkeeper: Small business needs bookkeeper with experience in automated bookkeeping systems. Must have two years technical education and training with associate degree preferred. Flex time and day care available. Salary $18,000 to $25,000. E.O.E.

The Tech-Prep/Associate-Degree Program in Action

Several community college and high-school systems are beginning to talk about and experiment with the 2 + 2 tech-prep/associate-degree program or similar articulation arrangements. Two such programs come from Newport News, Virginia, in the east and Bakersfield, California, in the west.

Virginia

Under the leadership of Thomas Kubala, President of Thomas Nelson Community College in Virginia, the leaders of the Peninsula Public Secondary Schools and the Peninsula Vocational-

153

Technical Center came together with the leaders of the community college to establish a four-year technical-education curriculum designed to prepare technicians for new advanced-technology occupations such as electronic and telecommunication technicians. The emphasis was placed upon a comprehensive and coordinated tech-prep/associate-degree curriculum spanning grades eleven through fourteen.

The aim of the program is to develop master technicians who are broadly educated. An interdisciplinary approach to technician education is utilized as well as a competency-based (CBE) component. The secondary-school program develops basic proficiencies in mathematics, applied sciences, communication skills, and trains students to apply these basic disciplines to tools, materials, processors, controls, and energy-conversion systems.

Figure 22

Postsecondary Curriculum Structure—General Philosophy

SPECIALTY AREA	• • • • Six courses selected • for specialization in • appropriate Hi-Tech area •	SPECIALIZATION
TECHNICAL CORE AREA	• Electricity • Fluids • Electronics • Thermics • Mechanics • Graphics • Electromechanics • Controls • Materials • Computers	COMMON CORE
BASIC SKILLS AREA	• Mathematics • Computer Literacy • Science • Socioeconomics • Communications	

Source: Leno S. Pedrotti, "Redesigning Vocational Curricula—Postsecondary Curriculum Design Guidelines,." Presentation at the American Vocational Association/Center for Occupational Research and Development Regional Workshop, Harpers Ferry, West Virginia, May 3–4, 1983.

The program is designed so that students can progress smoothly from the preparatory high-school level to a specific, yet flexible, technician program at the community college. The community college program consists of three parts: a common core of learning, a technical core of learning, and several specialty sequences. Figures 22 through 25 are models for the structure of such a postsecondary program.

The initial target population for this technician program included the senior-high-school students who were enrolled in the occupational areas of Clerk Typist and Related Occupations, Mechanical Drafting, and Machine Shop. The faculty, counselors, and administrators of the participating institutions who were responsible for the above-mentioned program areas were also directly involved in the program.

Schools	Number of Students Involved
Hampton City Schools	1500
Newport News City Schools	2400
Poquoson City Schools	136
Williamsburg-James City County Public Schools	164
York County Public Schools	300
Peninsula Vo-Tech	100
Thomas Nelson Community College	500
Total	5090

A written agreement was executed between the community college and the other participating schools. A sample of such an agreement follows:

Articulation Agreement

This agreement is made between Thomas Nelson Community College and Hampton City School Division.

We hereby agree to the following:

1. Participating instructors at the secondary and postsecondary level will formally adopt and teach from a list of competencies (task list) based on job entry-level task require-

155

Figure 23
Postsecondary Technology Curricula

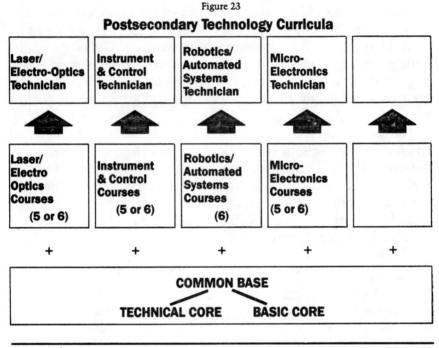

Source: Pedrotti.

ments. Criteria for evaluation and recording levels of competency will also be formally adopted.

2. Prior to the beginning of each academic year, a meeting will be scheduled to review each occupational area and amend, as necessary, the occupational task lists, grading systems, recording forms, and objective reference tests or criterion-referenced measures to establish levels of competency. The directors of vocational education of each participating school division and the Virginia Peninsula Vocational-Technical Educational Center, the appropriate division chairman at Thomas Nelson Community College, program heads, supervisors, and teacher representatives (as required) will attend.

3. The school division will maintain a competency record for each student which identifies areas and levels of task achievement. This record will become a part of the stu-

Figure 24

Postsecondary Curriculum Model for Robotics/Automated Systems Technology

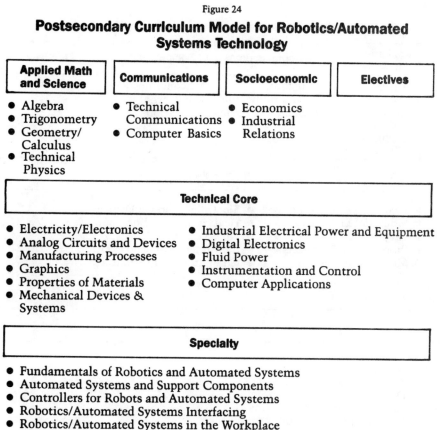

Applied Math and Science	Communications	Socioeconomic	Electives
• Algebra • Trigonometry • Geometry/ Calculus • Technical Physics	• Technical Communications • Computer Basics	• Economics • Industrial Relations	

Technical Core

- Electricity/Electronics
- Analog Circuits and Devices
- Manufacturing Processes
- Graphics
- Properties of Materials
- Mechanical Devices & Systems
- Industrial Electrical Power and Equipment
- Digital Electronics
- Fluid Power
- Instrumentation and Control
- Computer Applications

Specialty

- Fundamentals of Robotics and Automated Systems
- Automated Systems and Support Components
- Controllers for Robots and Automated Systems
- Robotics/Automated Systems Interfacing
- Robotics/Automated Systems in the Workplace
- Automated Work Cell Integration

Source: Pedrotti.

dent's official record and will be forwarded to Thomas Nelson Community College as part of the student's high-school transcript.

4. Credit at Thomas Nelson Community College will be granted for competencies mastered at an achievement level of 3.0 or better on a scale of 0-4, as defined in the respective instructional resource guides, providing continuation of study in the program area begins within two academic years after graduation from the secondary school.

157

Figure 25

Postsecondary Curriculum Model for Computer Technology

Applied Math and Science	Communications	Socioeconomic	Electives

• Algebra
• Trigonometry
• Geometry/
  Calculus
• Technical
  Physics
	• Technical
	  Communications
	• Computer Basics
		• Economics
		• Industrial
		  Relations	

Technical Core

• Electricity/Electronics
• Industrial Electricity
• Graphics
• Properties of Materials
• Mechanical Devices

• Electromechanical Devices
• Heating and Cooling
• Fluid Power
• Instrumentation and Control
• Computer Applications

Specialty

• Circuit Analysis
• Digital Fundamentals
• Active Devices and Circuits
• Digital Devices and Techniques
• Analog Devices and Systems
• Computer Circuits and Programming
• Digital Computers

Source: Pedrotti.

5. The college will provide a list of current courses for which advanced credit (in total or in part) applies.
6. No examinations will be required for granting credit for achievement of a competency and no fee will be required for advanced credit.
7. All participating new faculty and administrators, full-time and part-time, will have training in competency-based education and will receive orientation on the articulation process described herein.
8. This agreement will be reviewed annually as stated in number two above and, in addition, will be reviewed by

the President of Thomas Nelson Community College and the Superintendent of Hampton City School Division, or their designees, every three years.

President
Thomas Nelson
Community College

Superintendent of
Hampton City Schools

Date _____

Date _____

California
With the assistance of an employers advisory committee, the Kern High School District and the Kern Community College District have developed a 2 + 2 tech-prep/associate-degree program in agriculture education. Business-education coordination is also under development.

These two districts serve most of Kern County, California, and both have had agriculture programs for years. Kern County is one of the top three productive agriculture counties in the U.S. Agriculture accounts for about twenty percent of the wages and salaries earned in that region. The modern agribusiness enterprise finds itself in need of trained technicians in agriculture mechanics and in the application of computer science to production and marketing. Other needs relate to the training required in the use of chemical fertilizers, insecticides, and soil analysis.

The agriculture employers have been most critical of the high-school and college programs on two points: (1) they noted a significant lack of congruence between what is taught and what the agriculture industry needs, and (2) they were outspoken about the lack of communication within the educational institutions and with the agricultural employers of the county. With that impetus from the employers, the Boards of Trustees of the Kern High School District and Kern Community College District passed a joint resolution authorizing the formation of a joint advisory committee to make recommendations to the two districts with respect to the development of an agricultural instructional program that would be coordinated from high-school through community college level.

159

Under the leadership of Jim Young, Chancellor of the Kern Community College District, and Don Murfin, Superintendent of the Kern High School District, and key faculty members, along with the motivation of key agribusiness leaders, a 2 + 2 tech-prep/associate-degree program has been developed in Agriculture Business, Crop Science, Mechanized Agriculture, and Ornamental Horticulture. One of the interesting aspects of this program is the awarding of a competency certificate at the conclusion of each of the four years of study.

Other interesting features of this program include:

- A four-year emphasis on communication skills
- A four-year emphasis on mathematics and problem solving
- A greater depth of training in technical skills

Figure 26

Kern High School District and Kern Community College District Organizational Model

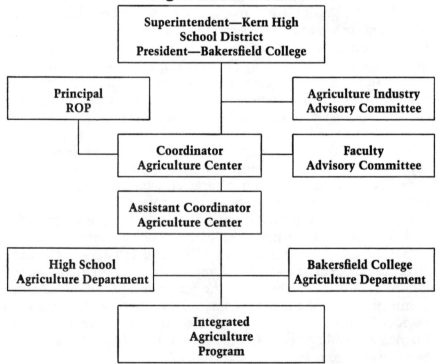

- Work experience opportunities as a result of job entry-level proficiencies
- An integrated introduction to the humanities and a common core of learning.

The Dallas County Community College District in Dallas, Texas, has been working for several years on coordinating the community college vocational-education programs with feeder high-school programs. Program articulation guides have been published in the following areas:

Auto mechanics   Building trades—carpentry
Child development   Digital electronics technology
Drafting and design technology   Legal assistant
Office careers   Medical lab technician

Figure 27

Kern High School District and Bakersfield College Agriculture Business

GRADE 11 FALL		GRADE 12 FALL		GRADE 13 FALL		GRADE 14 FALL	
COURSES	SITE	COURSES	SITE	COURSES	SITE	COURSES	SITE
American History	HS	American Government	HS	English-Composition (3)	BC	*English-Technical	
English	HS	English	HS	Humanities (3)	BC	Writing (3)	BC
Mathematics	HS	Conversational Span.	HS	Ag. Bus. 5—Ag.		Behavioral Science (3)	BC
Physical Science or		P.E. or Elective	HS	Computers (3)	BC/C	Physical Fitness	BC
Chemistry	HS	Technical Math (3)	C	Acctg. 53A Intro. to		Ag. Bus. 7—Calif.	
Typing/Comp. Intro.	ROP	Ag. Bus. 3—Ag. Mkt.		Accounting (3)	BC	Agriculture Law	BC
Ag. Bus. 1—Intro. to		& Econ. (3)	BC/C	Elective (3)	BC/C	Elective (3)	BC/C
Cal. Ag. (3)	BC/C						
GRADE 11 SPRING		**GRADE 12 SPRING**		**GRADE 13 SPRING**		**GRADE 14 SPRING**	
COURSES	SITE	COURSES	SITE	COURSES	SITE	COURSES	SITE
American History	HS	American Government	HS	English-Speech (3)	BC	Humanities (3)	BC
English	HS	English	HS	Ag. Bus. 6—Ag. Labor		Fine Arts (3)	BC
Mathematics	HS	Conversational Span.	HS	Relations (3)	BC	Mgnt. 59 Personnel	
Physical Science or		P.E. or Elective	HS	Physical Fitness (1)	BC	Management (3)	BC
Chemistry	HS	Technical Math (3)	C	Acctg. 53B (3) to		Elective (3)	BC
Typing/Computer	ROP	Ag. Bus. 4—Ag. Acctg.		Accounting	BC	Elective (3)	BC
Ag. Bus. 2—Ag. Bus.		& Farm Mngt. (3)	BC/C	Elective (3)	BC/C		
Management (3)	BC/C						
Certificate of competency in typing		High School diploma and/or certificate of competency in agriculture		Certificate of competency in the use of computers in agriculture		Associate of science degree in agriculture business	
Diploma/Certificate/Degree							

SUGGESTED ELECTIVES

AN. S. 1—Intro. to Animal Husbandry
AN. S. 2—Beef Production
AN. S. 3—Sheep Production
CRP. S. 1—Principles Crop Production
CRP. S. 2—Alfalfa & For. Crops
CRP. S. 3—Trees & Vines

CRP. S. 4—Advanced Trees & Vines
MECH. AG. 1—Intro. Agric. Mech.
Mech. Ag. 2—Ag. Equipment Ser. & Oper.
Ornamental Horticulture 2—Nursery Mgmt.
Ornamental Horticulture 3—Plant I.D.
Orn. Hort. 4—Plant Identification

Bus. A. 1A—Principles of Accounting (3)
Bus. A. 1B—Principles of Accounting (3)
Acctg. 54—Payroll Accounting (3)
Acctg. 3—Tax Accounting
Bus. A. 18A—Business Law (3)
Insur. 21—Principles of Insurance (3)

*Courses to be designed

Where courses will be taught (site):   **No. of college units indicated in: ( )**
Agriculture Center—C
Bakersfield College—BC
High School Campus—HS
Regional Occupational Program—ROP

Welding technology

Ornamental horticulture

Auto body technology

technology

These guides identify the competencies a student must possess to receive credit for specified courses in the community colleges.

There is much activity across the nation directed toward program coordination. The Illinois State Board of Education has spent considerable effort over the past two years in attempting to clarify the relationship between the secondary and postsecondary vocational-education delivery systems. By July 1, 1987, regional secondary-school systems and the community colleges must meet and define articulation agreements and/or cooperative arrangements.

Figure 28

Kern High School District and Bakersfield College Crop Science

GRADE 11 FALL		GRADE 12 FALL		GRADE 13 FALL		GRADE 14 FALL	
COURSES	SITE	COURSES	SITE	COURSES	SITE	COURSES	SITE
American History	HS	American Government	HS	English-Composition	BC	English	BC
English	HS	English	HS	Humanities	BC	Behavioral Science (2)	BC
Mathematics	HS	Conversational	HS	Crop.S 3—Trees &		Physical Fitness (1)	BC
Physical Science or		Spanish		Vines	C	Crop.S.5—Weed	
Chemistry	HS	P.E. or Elective	HS	Ag. Bus. 2—Ag. Bus.		Control (3)	C
Typing/Computer		Crop.S. 1—Prin. of		Management (3)	BC	Crop.S. 6—Soils (3)	C
Intro.	ROP	Crop Production (3)	C	Elective (3)	BC/C	Elective (3)	BC/C
Ag. Bus.1—Intro. to							
Cal. Ag. (3)	C						
GRADE 11 SPRING		GRADE 12 SPRING		GRADE 13 SPRING		GRADE 14 SPRING	
COURSES	SITE	COURSES	SITE	COURSES	SITE	COURSES	SITE
American History	HS	American Government	HS	English-Speech (3)	BC	Humanities (3)	BC
English	HS	English	HS	Crop.S. 4—Ad. Trees		Fine Arts (3)	BC
Mathematics	HS	Conversational	HS	Crops & Vines (3)	C	Physical Fitness (1)	BC
Physical Science or		Spanish		Mech. Ag. 6—Farm		Crop.S. 8—	C
Chemistry	HS	P.E. or Elective	HS	Fabrication (3)	C	Entomology (3)	C
Crop.S. 7—Irrigation (3)	C	Crop.S Math (3)	C	Elective (3)	BC/C	Mech. Ag. 3—Farm	
Mech. Ag. 2—Equip.		Crop.S. 2—Alfalfa &		Elective (3)	BC/C	Power (3)	C
Ser. & Opr. (3)	C	For. Crop (3)	C			Elective (3)	BC/C
Typing/Computer							
Intro.	ROP						
Certificate of competency in typing		High school diploma and/or certificate of competency in field crops production upon completion of grade 12 spring semester		Certificate of competency in tree and vine crops at the end of grade 13		Associate of science degree in crop production certificate in agronomy	
Diploma/Certificate/Degree							

SUGGESTED ELECTIVES

Agriculture Business 3—Agriculture Marketing & Economics
Agriculture Business 4—Accounting & Farm Management
Agriculture Business 5—Agriculture Computers
Agriculture Business 6—Agriculture Labor Relations
Animal Science 1—Introduction to Animal Science
Mechanized Agriculture 4—Farm Engines

Mechanized Agriculture 5—Fluid & Pneumatic Power
Mechanized Agriculture 7—Farm Tractors
Mechanized Agriculture 8—Farm Small Engines
Ornamental Horticulture 1—Plant Propagation
Welding 1—Oxy/Acetylene
Welding 538—ARC

Where courses will be taught (site)
Agriculture Center—C
Bakersfield College—BC
High School Campus—HS
Regional Occupational Program—ROP

For many years the Hagerstown Junior College in Hagerstown, Maryland, has maintained program-coordination agreements with feeder high schools in the areas of business education/secretarial science, licensed practical nursing/associate-degree nursing, distributive education/cooperative education. Three different types of procedures are followed in assessing competence: advanced placement, awarding college credit, and challenge examinations. Students following the articulation agreements have been tracked as they complete the associate-degree program. They make higher grades than those not following the articulation program and they tend to complete degree requirements earlier.

Finally, Sacramento City College President Doug Burris (now serving as Los Rios District's Vice Chancellor) and Sacramento

Figure 29

Kern High School District and
Bakersfield College Mechanized Agriculture

GRADE 11 FALL		GRADE 12 FALL		GRADE 13 FALL		GRADE 14 FALL	
COURSES	SITE	COURSES	SITE	COURSES	SITE	COURSES	SITE
American History	HS	American Government	HS	English—Composition	BC	English-Technical	
English	HS	English	HS	(3)	BC	Writing (3)	BC
Mathematics	HS	Conversational		Humanities (3)		Behavioral Science (3)	BC
Physical Science or		Spanish	HS	Mech. Ag. 5—Fluid	C	Physical Fitness (1)	BC
Chemistry	HS	P.E. or Elective	C	Pneumatic Power (3)	BC	Mech. Ag. 7—Farm	
Ag. Bus. 1—Intro. to		Technical Math (3)		Welding 538—ARC (3)	BC	Tractors (3)	C
Cal. Ag. (3)	C	Mech. Ag. 3—Farm	C	Auto 1—Basic Auto (3)	BC/C	Elective (3)	BC/C
		Power (3)		Elective (3)		Elective (3)	BC/C
GRADE 11 SPRING		**GRADE 12 SPRING**		**GRADE 13 SPRING**		**GRADE 14 SPRING**	
COURSES	SITE	COURSES	SITE	COURSES	SITE	COURSES	SITE
American History	HS	American Government	HS	English-Speech (3)	BC	Humanities (3)	BC
English	HS	English	HS	Mech. Ag. 6—Farm		Fine Arts (3)	BC
Mathematics	HS	Conversational		Fabrication (3)	C	Physical Fitness (1)	BC
Physical Science or		Spanish	HS	Mach. Shop 1—Elem.		Mech. Ag. 8—Farm	
Chemistry	HS	P.E. or Elective	HS	(3)	BC/C	Small Engines (3)	C
Mech. Ag. 1—Intro. to		Technical Math (3)	C	Elective (3)	BC/C	Elective (3)	BC/C
Ag. Mech. (3)	C	Mech. Ag. 4—Farm		Elective (3)			
Mech. Ag. 2—Equip.		Engines (3)	C				
Ser. & Opr. (3)	C						
Certificate of competency in service and operation upon completion of grade 11, spring semester		**High school diploma and/or certificate of competency in entry level farm mechanics**		**Certificate of competency in fabrication and repair**		**Associate of science degree in mechanized agriculture**	
Diploma/Certificate/Degree							

SUGGESTED ELECTIVES

Agriculture Business 2—Agriculture Business Management
Agriculture Business 5—Agriculture Computers
Animal Science 1—Introduction to Animal Science
Crop. S. 1—Principles of Crop Production
Crop. S. 3—Trees & Vines
Crop. S. 6—Soils
Crop. S. 7—Irrigation

Crop. S. 8—Entomology
Ornamental Horticulture 4—Plant Identification
Automobile 102 B—Automobile Engines Machinery
Machine Shop 53D—Advanced Machine Shop
Mechanical Technical 59A—Basic Hydraulic Fluid Mechanical
Welding 1—Oxy/Acetylene
Welding 74—Tig and Mig

Where courses will be taught (site):
Agriculture Center—C
Bakersfield College—BC
High School Campus—HS
Regional Occupational Program—ROP

No. of college units indicated in: ( )

163

City Unified School District Superintendent Tom Guigni have created the Sacramento City College-Sacramento City Unified School District Articulation Council. The Council is composed of administrators, including deans of instruction from each segment, who meet monthly. Special articulation committees work in the following areas: English; English as a Second Language; Counseling Services; Occupational Technology; Math, Science, and Computers; Core Assessment. Soon to become involved are Humanities, Fine Arts, and Social Sciences.

Four objectives were set for the project: to integrate the two systems' curriculum; to develop a core assessment/placement

Figure 30

Kern High School District and Bakersfield College Ornamental Horticulture

GRADE 11 FALL		GRADE 12 FALL		GRADE 13 FALL		GRADE 14 FALL	
COURSES	SITE	COURSES	SITE	COURSES	SITE	COURSES	SITE
American History	HS	American Government	HS	English—Composition	BC	English-Technical (3)	BC
English	HS	English	HS	(3)		Behavorial Science (3)	BC
Mathematics	HS	Conversational		Humanities	BC	Physical Science (3)	BC
Physical Science or		Spanish	HS	Orn. Hort. 4—Plant		Orn. Hort. 6—	
Chemistry	HS	P.E. or Elective	HS	Identification (3)	BC	Landscape Cont./	
Ag. Bus. 1—Intro. to		Technical Math (3)	C	Crop. S. 6—Soils (3)	C	Maint. (3)	BC
Cal. Ag. (3)	C	Ag. Bus. 2—Ag. Bus.		Mech. Ag. 1—Intro. to		Crop. S. 7—Irrigation (3)	C
		Management (3)	BC	Ag. Mech. (3)	C	Mech. Ag. 6—Farm	
						Fabrication (3)	C
GRADE 11 SPRING		**GRADE 12 SPRING**		**GRADE 13 SPRING**		**GRADE 14 SPRING**	
COURSES	SITE	COURSES	SITE	COURSES	SITE	COURSES	SITE
American History	HS	American Government	HS	English-Speech (3)	BC	Humanities (3)	BC
English	HS	English	HS	Orn. Hort. 5—Land.		Fine Arts (3)	BC
Mathematics	HS	Conversational		Design (3)	BC	Physical Fitness (1)	BC
Physical Science or		Spanish	HS	Crop. S. 8—		Orn. Hort. 7—Turf	
Chemistry	HS	P.E. or Elective	HS	Entolomogy (3)	C	Management (3)	BC
Orn. Hort. 1—Plant-		Technical Math (3)	C	Mech. Ag. 2—Ag.		Mech. Ag. 4—Farm	
Propagation (3)	BC	Orn. Hort. 3—Plant		Equip. Ser. & Oper. (3)		Engines (3)	C
Orn. Hort. 2—Nursery		Identification	BC	Ag. Bus. 3—Ag.	C	Ag. Bus. 5—Agricul-	
Management (3)	BC			Marketing		ture Computers (3)	BC
				& Economics (3)	BC	Elective (3)	BC/C
				Elective (3)	BC/C		
Certificate of competency in plant care and maintenance		High school diploma and/or certificate of competency in nursery management upon completion of grade 12 spring semester		Certificate of competency in landscape design		Associate of science degree in ornamental horticulture and/or certificate or competency in landscape maintenance/turf	
Diploma/Certificate/Degree							

SUGGESTED ELECTIVES

Agriculture Business 4—Agriculture Accounting & Farm
  Management
Agriculture Business 6—Agriculture Labor Relations
Crop. S. 5—Weed Control
Mechanical Agriculture 3—Farm Power

Mechanical Agriculture 5—Fluid & Pneumatic Power
Welding 1—Oxy/Acetylene
Welding 53B-ARC

Source: Kern Community College District

Where courses will be taught (site):
  Agriculture Center—C
  Bakersfield College—BC
  High School Campus—HS
  Regional Occupational Program—ROP

No. of college units indicated in: ( )

Figure 31

Dallas County Community College District—Student Profile

DALLAS COUNTY COMMUNITY COLLEGE DISTRICT
DIGITAL ELECTRONICS PROGRAM ARTICULATION
STUDENT PROFILE

School _____

Verification
Signature _____
School Official

Date _____

Student's Name	Birthdate		SS#	
Address	City	State		Zip

PLEASE TRANSMIT STUDENT PROFILE TO COLLEGE REGISTRAR AS SOON AS IT IS READY FOR EVALUATION.

	Date	Instructor's Signature
1. DC CIRCUITS		
Introduction to Electricity		
1.01 * Define terms of sketch symbols for terms related to electricity		
1.02 * List major characteristics of a substance which govern its conductance		
1.03 * Describe creation of a potential difference		
1.04 * List possible effects of applying a potential difference to a conductor		
1.05 * Describe an element		
1.06 * Draw schematic symbol for a battery and label polarity of terminals		
1.07 * List most common causes of laboratory accidents and ways to prevent them		
1.08 * List general precautions to prevent lab accidents		
1.09 * List steps to take if lab partner receives electrical shock		
1.10 * Practice good safety habits and correct laboratory procedures		
Voltage, Current, and Resistance		
1.11 * Define and sketch lab and formula symbols for voltage, amperage, and resistance		
1.12 * Describe electron current flow and conventional current flow philosophies and state difference between them		
1.13 * List the 4 factors affecting conductor resistance and state how each affects the resistance		
1.14 * Prepare for reading resistors		
1.15 * Read values of 10 resistors		
1.16 * Identify linear and nonlinear portions of a scale		

continued

165

Figure 31

Student Profile (continued)

	Date	Instructor's Signature
1. DC CIRCUITS (Continued)		
1.17 · Identify value of picket		
1.18 · Define knob terms		
Scientific Notation and Metric Prefixes		
1.19 · Convert numbers		
1.20 · Complete test on number forms		
1.21 · Define and write symbol for metric prefix terms		
1.22 · Read 20 standard four-banded color-coded resistors		
1.23 · Write standard color code for resistors		
Ohm's Law and Power		
1.24 · Calculate 20 Ohm's Law problems		
1.25 · Enter number into calculator		
1.26 · Perform mathematical operations with calculator		
1.27 · Predict effect on the unknown quantity		
1.28 · Convert schematic drawing into working circuit		
1.29 · Define "polarity" and list effects of incorrect polarity on voltmeter		
1.30 · List and use techniques for avoiding meter movement damage when using VOM		
1.31 · Read 6 voltage values from a VOM Scale		
1.32 · Pass test on VOM reading		
1.33 · Define and identify a series circuit		
1.34 · Describe behavior of voltage, current, and resistance in a series circuit		
1.35 · Pass test on unknown values of series circuit		
1.36 · Define terms related to series circuits		
1.37 · Construct a series circuit with ammeter and read current value		
Introduction to Parallel Circuits		
1.38 · Pass test on unknown values of parallel resistances		
1.39 · Define terms related to parallel circuits		
1.40 · Describe the 3 laws governing parallel circuits		
1.41 · Calculate total resistance values of circuits with unlike resistors		
1.42 · Calculate total resistance of parallel circuit with two unlike resistors		
1.43 · Calculate total resistance value of circuit with several resistors of the same value		
1.44 · Calculate and measure value of resistance, current, and voltage		

Figure 31

Student Profile (continued)

	Date	Instructor's Signature
Parallel Circuit Analysis		
1.45 · Describe behavior of voltage, current, and resistance in a parallel circuit		
1.46 · Pass test on unknown values of parallel circuits		
1.47 · Calculate and measure total resistance of circuit		
Parallel-Series Circuits		
1.48 · Define and identify parallel-series circuit and series-parallel circuit		
1.49 · Reduce parallel-series circuit to one equivalent resistor		
1.50 · Reduce circuit to single resistor, and draw each equivalent circuit		
1.51 · Calculate all voltage and current values for each reduced circuit component		
1.52 · Calculate all unknown values in parallel-series circuits		
1.53 · Measure resistance, voltage, and current at any point in parallel circuit with four or more branches		
Series-Parallel Circuits		
1.54 · Reduce series-parallel circuit to one equivalent resistor		
1.55 · Reduce circuit to one equivalent resistor, showing each reduced circuit		
1.56 · State values of current and voltage for each resistor in original circuit		
1.57 · Calculate all unknown values of series-parallel circuits		
1.58 · Identify switches		
1.59 · Define terms related to series-parallel circuits		
1.60 · Connect two-way and three-way switching arrangements		
Voltage Dividers and Power		
1.61 · State the 9 formulas for power in a DC circuit		
1.62 · Write lab and formula symbols for power in electrical circuit		
1.63 · Define "one watt of electrical power"		
1.64 · Define and perform, with a calculator, "squaring a number" and "square root of a number"		
1.65 · Pass power test		
1.66 · Calculate voltage, current, and resistance for all parts of circuit and prove calculations		

Source: Dallas County Community College District

The student must complete the 66 core (·) competencies.

model; to plan an articulation program for instructional programs and students services; and to disseminate information about these activities. Some accomplishments of the council thus far:

- A process to exchange course outlines, teaching materials, faculty rosters, and educational films
- Curriculum guides for teachers and students
- Articulation agreements which specify student competency levels
- An inter-institutional directory of English teachers.

Additionally, the Sacramento articulation project has been regarded as a vehicle for assessment and research on student performance and learning problems, as well as a colloquium for teachers. The Articulation Council has extended the college's comprehensive assessment testing program to selected groups of students in the high schools, evaluated the results, and formed a permanent Research and Evaluation Committee.

Some Suggestions for Cultivating Excellence

In the conditions of modern life, the rule is absolute. The race which does not value trained intelligence is doomed. Today we maintain ourselves. Tomorrow science will have moved forward yet one more step, and there will be no appeal from the judgment which will be pronounced on the uneducated.

Alfred North Whitehead

It is important to review the major focus of this book. It is not a book about the comprehensive high schools. It is not a book about the comprehensive community colleges. No attempt has been made to review the comprehensive mission of these great American institutions. The college-prep/baccalaureate-degree program remains an important part of the high-school and community college programs. However, this book throws the spotlight upon some real-life people called "ordinary students" and upon how high schools and community colleges might work together on behalf of this middle quartile of students. The non-baccalaureate-degree students deserve and need an excellent education—and in most cases require a better education than they are now experiencing. By and large the education reform reports are silent on this subject.

Excellence in education will not be achieved by pronouncements, politics, or postulates. It will not even be achieved by pursuit of excellence. Excellence in education cannot be caught. It can only be cultivated, challenged, and celebrated.

To pursue means to follow for the purpose of overtaking or capturing—to chase something. It is not uncommon to hear school and college personnel talk about the pursuit of excellence as though excellence were an object to be caught. The metaphor is inappropriate. How many educators across the land are breathless from chasing an elusive excellence?

To cultivate means to prepare for growth—to promote or improve the growth of something by labor and attention. How many times have you heard schools and colleges use the slogan "Cultivating Excellence"? My guess is not often. *Here is the crucial question: Is your school or college chasing excellence or cultivating excellence?*

Whether a high school sends all or most of its students to college; whether a community college specializes in university-

171

parallel courses, or technical education, or developmental education; whether a university stresses professional courses over the liberal arts; whether the students are old or young, black or white, full time or part time, are not the issues in cultivating excellence in education. *What does matter is how faithfully schools and colleges are seeking the best in all their students rather than in just some of them, and how closely they are following their own institutional beliefs, articles of faith, and sense of mission.*

How do we evaluate an excellent society? By the computers in our businesses, the cars in our garages, the money in our banks? I think not. *History will gauge this generation primarily by what we have done with our human resources and our human values. If we do not cultivate the best in our people and fully utilize our human resources, we become a wasteful society regardless of what else we do.*

The waste of our human resources is not only a national embarrassment, but in a rapidly changing world it is also a threat to the United States, placing it at a disabling disadvantage in the world economic competition. In many ways, our economic system has been extraordinarily successful. But let us not be fooled by past successes into thinking that we can continue to waste our most precious resources. The path to the Great Society was "more of everything." We are now learning, the hard way, that quantity is no substitute for quality. Any new attempt to revitalize our economy or our educational system will fall far short of its goal unless we place a high value upon cultivating excellence and the full development of our human resources.

How do we begin to ensure that excellence is cultivated in our schools and colleges? We are advocating that roundtable discussions be initiated across the country, with high-school and community college leaders developing local plans of action for cooperative efforts. The continuity and coherence of a student's education depends in large measure upon the success of such a venture. Seven specific recommendations are offered here for consideration in these discussions:

1. All students need a *student-centered curriculum.*

We must rethink our definition of excellence in high schools and colleges. Can one program or one definition of excellence be applicable for all aspects of education and for all students? Can we develop winners from ordinary people as well as from the academically talented and gifted? Or is education only a process of sorting out and selecting the winner? We must begin to identify and remove the barriers to achieving excellence in education for *all* students. What are some barriers in your schools and colleges?

2. All students must experience *greater structure and substance* in their educational programs.

When all the rhetoric is blown away from the various reports on improving education, one would not be far off the mark to summarize the recommendations as calling for greater structure and more substance in the high school. Unfocused learning simply will not produce excellence. How much unfocused learning is going on in your schools and colleges?

3. Students must see *coherence* in their educational programs.

Clear signals must be given high-school faculty, students, and their parents about the role of preparatory requirements for succeeding in a community, technical, or junior college. Open admissions and open doors cannot be interpreted to mean that preparation is unimportant. Much greater attention must be given the exit requirements of these colleges in communicating with high-school students. Much greater attention must also be given to coherence in the curriculum, calling for closer program articulation between high schools and colleges. How much program coordination is going on between your high school and the community college? How much do your students know about associate degrees?

4. Students must see *connectedness* between what they do and the larger whole—between education and the rest of the real world.

It is time to review the concept of career education. Such a review may provide the connecting link between the liberal arts and vocational education as well as a new definition of excellence in education. The walls must come down between vocational education and the liberal arts. Students preparing to meet the demands of the information age need both. Can a tech-prep/associate-degree program help provide connectedness?

5. Students must experience *continuity* in learning.

The loss of continuity in learning is profound for many students. This loss is often the result of a highly mobile society where people move from one community to another. More often, loss of continuity in learning can be attributed to student absenteeism or to just plain disinterest in the school program. However, schools and colleges must share some of the blame for loss of continuity in learning. Little attention has been given to the connecting links and coordination of the curriculum between high schools and colleges. Although the reform reports give little attention to this subject, loss of continuity in learning may be one of the significant barriers to achieving excellence in education. Can a clearly focused tech-prep/associate-degree program prevent loss of continuity in learning?

6. Students must be offered a larger range of *choices*, so that their lives and work are not unnecessarily degrading, or boring, or limiting.

The information age and the demands of technical education require some new thinking about the vocational-technical programs in high schools and community colleges. The high-school vocational-education curriculum must aim at preparing students for broad careers rather than for specific jobs. This book recommends a 2 + 2 tech-prep/associate-degree approach for at least some students. What is the program for your non-baccalaureate-degree-bound students?

7. Students must see the necessity to *continue to learn*

throughout a lifetime to avoid obsolescence and to develop the competencies to become life-long learners.

Community, technical, and junior colleges have come of age. It is time to recognize these institutions as colleges of excellence and to value the role they play in meeting the life-long learning needs of an adult America. It is fundamental to the schooling process that it help individuals to develop the capacity to grow and to change throughout their lives. How much do your high-school students know about life-long learning and the opportunities found in community colleges?

Excellence in education is inevitably linked to the larger issue of human-resource development in our country. If we do not know how to seek the best in *all* our citizens and to fully utilize our human resources, we become a wasteful society regardless of what we do elsewhere.

References

Adelman, Clifford. 1983. Devaluation, diffusion and the college connection. Unpublished paper prepared for the National Commission on Excellence in Education.

———. 1984. The school-college connection. *NASSP Bulletin*. October, 5-18.

American Enterprise Institute for Public Policy Research. 1983. Women, welfare and enterprise. Conference, Washington, D.C.

Armbrister, Trevor. 1985. The teacher who took on the establishment. *Reader's Digest* March, 23-28.

Association of American Colleges. 1985. Integrity in the college curriculum: a report to the academic community.

Astin, Alexander. 1982. The American college freshman, 1966-81. Commissioned paper for the National Commission on Excellence in Education.

Boyer, Ernest. 1985. *High School*. New York: Harper and Row, Colophon ed.

Cohen, Arthur. 1984-85. Helping ensure the right to succeed: an ERIC review. *Community College Review* 12:4-9.

Coleman, James S. 1972. The children have outgrown the schools. *Psychology Today* February, 72-84.

Coleman, William et al. 1983. Educating Americans for the 21st century. National Science Board Commission on Pre-College Education in Mathematics, Science and Technology. Washington, D.C.: Government Printing Office.

Cross, K. Patricia. 1984. Societal imperatives: need for an educated democracy. Unpublished paper presented at the National Conference on Teaching and Excellence, Austin, Texas.

Echternacht, G. J. 1976. Characteristics distinguishing vocational education students from general and academic students. *Multivariate Behavior Research* 11:477-490.

Ehrenreich, Barbara and Karen Stallard. 1982. The nouveau poor. *Ms. Magazine* July/August, 217-224.

Fetters, William. 1975. National longitudinal study of the high-school class of 1972: student test results by sex, high-school program, ethnic category and father's education. Washington, D.C.: National Center for Education Statistics.

Frankl, Victor E. 1984. *Man's search for meaning*. New York: Washington Square Press, 1963.

Gardner, David P. et al. 1983. *A nation at risk: the imperative for educational reform*. National Commission on Excellence in Education. Washington, D.C.: Government Printing Office.

Gardner, John W. 1984. *Excellence*. New York: Harper and Row, 1961.

Goldhammer, Keith and Robert Taylor. 1972. *Career education, perspective and promise*. New York: Charles E. Merrill.

Grant, W. Vance and Leo J. Eden. 1982. *Digest of Education Statistics, 1981*. National Center for Education Statistics. Washington, D.C.: Government Printing Office.

Hechinger, Fred M. 1984. School-college collaboration—an essential to improved public education. *NASSP Bulletin* October, 69-79.

Honig, Bill. 1985. The educational excellence movement: now comes the hard part. *Kappan* June, 675-681.

Kelly, James J. 1983. Freshman survey. Unpublished paper. Pennsylvania State University.

Koltai, Leslie. 1984. *Redefining the associate degree*. Washington, D.C.: American Association of Community and Junior Colleges.

Levine, Sol. 1984. College admission requirements and the high-school program. *NASSP Bulletin* October, 19-25.

Maslow, Abraham. 1954. *Motivation and personality*. New York: Harper and Row.

Moore, David. 1984. The English educational system. Unpublished paper presented to Regional and Community Colleges as Agents of Change: An International Symposium, Negev, Israel.

Naisbitt, John. 1984. *Megatrends*. New York: Warner Books.

_____. 1984. *The year ahead: 1985*. Washington, D.C.: The Naisbitt Group.

National Commission on Secondary Vocational Education. 1984. The unfinished agenda: the role of vocational education in the high school. National Center for Research in Vocational Education, Ohio State University.

Occupational Outlook Handbook, 1984-85 ed. Bureau of Labor Statistics. Washington, D.C.: Government Printing Office.

Pedrotti, Leno S. 1983. Redesigning vocational criteria—postsecondary curriculum design guidelines. Unpublished paper presented at American Vocational Association/Center for Occupational Research and Development regional workshop, Harpers Ferry, West Virginia.

Peng, Samuel S., William B. Fetters and Andrew J. Kolstad. 1983. A capsule description of high-school students. High school and beyond: a national longitudinal study for the 1980's. National Center for Education Statistics. Washington, D.C.: Government Printing Office.

Plesko, Valena White and Joyce D. Stern, eds. 1985. *The condition of education 1985*. National Center for Education Statistics. Washington, D.C.: Government Printing Office.

Press, Pat. 1984. It's not dirty work. *Washington Post* May 27.

Pyatt, Rudolph A. Jr. 1985. On jobs in the future. *Washington Post* March 8.

Raspberry, William. 1984. Skimming the underclass. *Washington Post* November 28. © 1984, Washington Post Writers Group. Reprinted with permission.

Riday, George, Ronald Bingham and Thomas Harvey. 1984-85. Satisfaction of community college faculty: exploding a myth. *Community College Review* 12:46-50.

Two years after high school: a capsule description of 1980 seniors. 1984. High school and beyond: a national longitudinal study for the 1980's. National Center for Education Statistics. Washington, D.C.: Government Printing Office.

Vaughan, George. 1983. Historical perspective: President Truman endorsed community college manifesto. *Community and Junior College Journal* April, 24.

Wagenaar, Theodore. 1981. High school seniors' view of themselves and their schools: a trend analysis. *Kappan* September, 29-32.

Washington Post 1985. Flaws in education of Hispanics cited. January 29.

Washington Post 1985. Jobless rate dips to 7.3%. March 9.

Washington Post 1985. February 2.

Weinstein, Robert V. 1983. *Jobs for the 21st century*. New York: Macmillan, Collier Books.

Whitlock, Baird. 1978. *Don't hold them back*. New York: College Entrance Examination Board.

Young, John A. 1985. Defining education to fit the advances of the future. Spring High Tech '85, *Washington Post*, May 5.

Index of Proper Names and Institutions

181